how to write a love letter that works

The Whens, Whys and Hows of Expressing Terms of Endearment

Sidney Bernstein and Linda Tarleton

SHAPOLSKY PUBLISHERS, INC.
NEW YORK

A Shapolsky Book

For any additional information, contact:
Shapolsky Publishers, Inc.
136 West 22nd Street, New York, NY 10011
(212) 633-2022

10 9 8 7 6 5 4 3 2 1

Library of Congress Cataloging-in-Publication Data

Bernstein, Sidney, 1938–
   How to write a love letter that works: the whens, whys and hows of
expressing terms of endearment / Sidney Bernstein and Linda Tarleton.
    p.   cm.
   ISBN 1-56171-003-2
   1. Love-letters. I. Tarleton, Linda, 1937–   . II. Title.
HQ801.3.B47   1991
395'. 4—dc20   90-47009

Printed and bound by Graficromo s.a., Cordoba, Spain

To that great lady Joyce Elaine Bernstein, who has shared my life both near and far—with gratitude for her two treasured gifts: Michael and Sherry.

And to Andra Jane Schutz, for climbing the mountain with me to see Opaekaa Falls and strolling the beaches at Hanalei, Lumahai, and Ke'e, and for understanding why I count robins.

Twice in a lifetime, you really fall in love.

Sid

To Ryan and Drew, and Tyler, too—with special thanks to Ryan for all his best colors.

With love,

Linda

A C K N O W L E D G M E N T S

Their Feelings

Professor Theodore Silver of Touro Law Center, Huntington, New York, midwived this book. The author of a variety of instructional books himself, his guidance assured that the book would be more than merely a collection of the authors' love letters. Rather, we were able to produce a work that will enable our readers to create their own love letters and, we hope, strengthen their own relationships.

To Jenifer Latham, who prepared the many drafts of the manuscript, no thanks could possibly be sufficient.

His Feelings

Three dear friends read many of these chapters and generously shared their insights and advice: Ilana Tolpin (the friend mentioned in Chapter 5) and Lynn Schwartz, both of New York City, and Myra Shuster, Esq., of Montreal. Some of the most important letters were initially written to Lynn and to Myra. I still mean every word of them.

To Chris Hess (née Loupy), wherever she may be, who taught me the meaning of the word "love." And, finally, acknowledgments are due Arleen Korn West, my high school sweetheart, whom I encountered again after more than thirty years, for teaching me that it is never too late to fall in love.

Her Feelings

Acknowledgments are due to my patient family and friends— whom I seldom see, lately—for their encouragement and faith, to Brighton Beach . . . and to lovers everywhere.

C O N T E N T S

We believe that open, honest, effective communication is the secret of building and maintaining rewarding relationships. We also believe that in a world of mobile telephones and clattering fax machines, headline summaries, and sound bites, most people have lost the art of expressive communication. With all the advantages of modern communication technology, something in the poetry, the imagery of language has been lost.

There was a time when writing a love letter was an established form of courtship. It was an age of romanticism and there was a certain beauty to it. While the forms of expression used in those days would now be considered archaic, the ideas are universal. A return to what was good in the past is not old-fashioned if it is updated to account for modern times and trends.

That's what we have set out to do in this book: introduce you to the modern love letter, though the situations in which you will make use of it are as old as relationships themselves. Times change, but the feelings of lovers are the same today as ever.

You will note that most of the chapters set forth "His Feelings" and "His Letter," followed by "Her Feelings" and "Her Letter." Part of the reason for this is a recognition that men and women may well view relationship problems differently. A larger part of the reason for the 'Feelings" sections, however, is simply to make the point that the authors are distinct individuals with their own backgrounds, histories, and personalities. Any two people will look at these situations somewhat differently.

It is important that you understand this. You may well choose to copy a sentence or a phrase from a particular letter. But we caution you not to copy an entire letter and send it out over your name. To make one of our letters effective, you have to filter what we have said through the prism of your own personality. You can adapt but you cannot adopt! Your experiences are different from ours and the recipients of your letters differ from the recipients of ours. In short, our letters may start the creative juices flowing and may start you thinking—and the advice we give you in a "P.S." following each series of letters should be taken seriously—but your letter must be a reflection of you, your life and experience, not of us or ours.

So go out and buy some beautiful stationery and a colored pen to match, stop by the post office and get a supply of their new "love" stamps, and start writing. You'll know your love letter "works" if you are able to effectively and persuasively communicate your feelings in such a manner that your beloved understands not only *how* you feel but *why*—and what those feelings mean for both of you.

Good luck. And drop us a line now and then.

Sidney Bernstein
Nyack-on-Hudson, New York
September 1990

Why Write a Love Letter?

Why write a love letter? For the same reasons you write any letter: to promote understanding between two people, to strengthen the bonds of the relations that exist between you. How nice it would be if we were telepathic so that our minds would bridge each other's, so that all we felt toward another person could be conveyed to them instantly, in all its intensity and, most important, accurately, so that there could be no possibility that our feelings could be misunderstood. Because *understanding* is the true intent of communication.

Our modern technology certainly allows instant communication worldwide, but impersonal devices can't accomplish "understanding" for us. Letters can, when they are written properly. After all, they have served that purpose for generations.

"But our relationship is great!"

Wonderful. Why not keep it that way? Who says you can't improve on a good thing? Even a diamond needs polishing now and then in order to retain its true luster. Some counselors claim they can improve a relationship that's not quite as good as it could be and make a good one better. So can you. With your letters. And a stamp costs only 25 cents.

Why do relationships go wrong? Usually it's because the parties begin to misunderstand each other and fail to correct the misunderstanding. Imagine a ship traveling one degree off course. On a short journey, this won't matter much. But if the navigator does not discover his error and travels hundreds of miles, his ship will make land far from its intended destination. On the other hand, if the navigator *does* discover his error before traveling too far, he corrects himself and puts the ship back on its proper course.

You want your relationship to continue on course over the long haul, not to be lost at sea. But a relationship lacking true communication, the *understanding* we describe in Chapter 2, is bound to go astray.

Why a love letter in either case—in a good relationship or in one that's slipping? Why not a phone call or a tête-à-tête in quiet surroundings? Simple. Good communication requires consideration, reflection, and craftsmanship. These are hard to achieve face-to-face, with the immediacy of the spoken word. Unless you are the world's greatest stage performer and a quick study to boot, you can't think and talk fast enough on your feet to get a clear message across to your partner, and have it understood exactly as you intend it to be. Neither can your partner in response. Your emotions get in the way. Letters written in reflection and with all the craftsmanship you possess are the best tool you can use to maintain the momentum of growth and development in your relationship.

Such letters permit you to (1) consider exactly what you wish to say; (2) consider best how to say it; (3) consider the person who will receive your letter; (4) reconsider what you have written; (5) edit if necessary; (6) decide whether or not to mail the letter.

We can hear you now: "I've never written a love letter in my life!" "I'm no romantic." "I can't even write a grocery list, much less a love letter." And, of course: "I haven't got the time."

Many people have never written a love letter. They are conditioned to picking out the greeting-card sentiment that suits their situation best. Often the preprinted words are way off the mark, but people make do, sign their love and kisses, and hope their feelings have been conveyed. We say you don't have to rely on these faulty tools anymore. And you don't have to be scared. Love letters aren't all that hard. In fact, they're pretty easy, once you decide to write only your honest feelings. And one love letter is much like another. Only the *circumstances* change. Once you've learned to do the backstroke in a pool, you can do it in a lake, a river, or an ocean. The conditions change a little—the water may be cool or salty, or there may be big waves or undercurrents. No matter. It's all water, and the stroke's the same. So jump right in. You are writing the history of your relationship and moving it forward.

Linda Tarleton
Port Washington, New York
September 1990

What Is This Thing Called *** ?

The mind is always the dupe of the heart.
—La Rochefoucauld, *Maxims*

e all want love. We spend years and decades searching for it—and more time, still, trying to make it last. Love means many things. It's someone to be with, someone to talk with, and someone to share our hopes, goals, and tastes with. Love is a partner. It is tenderness, compassion, and belonging. Love is, in the last analysis, that "special person."

To attract that special person, we spend not only time, but money. Industries package us for sale in a virtual market of love. They sell us silky hair, softer skin, sweeter scent, and sexy smiles. This, they promise, will bring us love. We believe them and we buy. We undergo costly, tortuous beauty treatments, men and women alike. We undergo peels, tucks, and surgical overhauls just to allure that special other. We read the pop periodicals and we ask ourselves: "Does My Body Still Excite Him?" "What Makes a Man a Turn-On?" "Will I Ever Be a Perfect 10?"

There's no doubt about it. When we meet someone, we see the physical features first. And when we think of ourselves, most of us have a physical image we want to perfect. Unfortunately, we also have in mind an idealized physical image of our "perfect other." When the physical aspect of a potential partner fits our image, we start to see through the "eyes of love." These are wishful eyes, with faulty vision. They actually believe that there is a perfect person, "made for us."

How ever did we come to think such a thing? For how long have we thought it? This is hard to say, but the idea of perfect union is expressed in so ancient a story as the Greek myth of the Androgynes. The Androgynes were idealized creatures: perfect beings in a perfect world until they were split in two by vicious Fate and doomed to search forever for their original other perfect half. The god Zeus, himself no slouch at love, took pity on the creatures and gave them sexuality for consolation and procreation.

Lovers fated for each other figure large in our literature and history, mostly in twos, sometimes in threes: Samson and Delilah, Jason and Medea (and Penelope), Lancelot and Guinevere (and Arthur), Laura and Petrarch, Héloïse and Abélard, Dante and Beatrice, Anthony and Cleopatra (and Julius Caesar) are a few. Their stories, fictional and real, blaze tempestuous passion through our literature and history. We accept the myth that real love is fire and ice, a "divine madness" between destined lovers.

Centuries of lovers and would-be lovers have tried to categorize love. To the ancient Greeks, Love was a primordial force, dominant in the universe until Strife appeared, an equal and opposing force. When peace and harmony were apparent, Love prevailed. When hate and disharmony existed, Strife held sway. The two forces ruled earth, air, fire, and water—and in turn our bodies and souls. The blood was believed to contain life and the heart to be the place where all elements were perfectly fused.

Therefore, what the heart desired couldn't be wrong. Little did they know.

In both Greece and Rome, love was channeled and divided neatly into categories: perfect friendship, platonic love, a union of the self with the whole, a union of the self with the divine, and erotic love. The concept of fated or "ideal" love was confined to the worship of perfect physical beauty in a perfect soul.

Conjugal love was legislated to death. Social status and profession determined whether and whom one could marry. Military men, as well as actors and prostitutes, were off-limits, the former presumably because marriage would be a distraction, the latter because they were not considered socially acceptable. Marriage, in all, was not highly regarded; it was at best "a combining of the pleasant with the useful." And neither were women, who were, at best, "valuable as preparers of food." Divorce was so common that Tertullian, a Roman historian, termed divorce the "consequence of marriage." Adultery and prostitution were rife, the institution of the family disintegrated, and the birth rate declined. With their male populations decimated by war and their governments unstable, Greece and Rome after long centuries made celibacy a crime. Adultery was severely punished. Marriage was obligatory for women under 50 and men under 60. Anyone older was considered better preoccupied with food and drink. Unmarried or divorced persons were heavily taxed, even disenfranchised. The value of love, even if imperfect, was reevaluated in not-so-grand-and-glorious Greece and Rome, but a little late.

Judaeo-Christianity emphasized other aspects of love: charity, brotherhood, forbearance, and tolerance—except toward women. The Old Testament still required wives to submit themselves to their husbands in all respects. The proverbial pearl of great price—the virtuous woman—was working so hard and long that she never would have had time for a flighty thought. Later, various Catholic saints classified women variously as defective and misbegotten, the devil's gateway, and unclean, a wife being "among the greatest of all evils." Their comment may have led to Chaucer's declaration that there was "no libel on women that the clergy will not paint."

Women didn't fare too well at all until the 12th Century with the advent of courtly love, a consequence of peaceful times, more money and leisure, and an influx of Arabic and Moorish music and thought into western Europe. Now women were adored by troubadours who praised their beauty in stylized *chansons*, or songs. The minstrels described men who, struck by love, were transformed by its powers from clods to noble suitors willing to give their all, to the death if need be, for a glance, a hankie, a token, a lock of hair. This languishing and unfulfilled ardor was considered perfect love. Love between married persons was considered impossible. Fidelity was considered possible only between lovers.

From the 13th Century to the 16th, the concept of love as a sacrament gained merit, with the plighting of troths, the proclaiming of marriage banns, and the necessity for ecclesiastical blessing of marital union. Fidelity was again prized and adultery a crime. Divorce was difficult, even forbidden. The social value of preserving union between the sexes and demanding ethical conduct from both was recognized as a way of preserving morality, the family, and social and civil harmony.

From the 17th Century to the 19th, views of love continued their revolution: restricted love, free love, sanctified love, romantic love. Century after century, in volume after volume, priests, poets, and philosophers tried to explain love, perfect or imperfect. Much later, Richard Rodgers would ask, "Who can?"

Not until the 20th Century did the concept of love become, at least in most of the Western World, one of equal partnership with the members of the union having equal right to gratification and security in it. We've come a long way—right? Unlike our ancestors, we know what love is and what we want. And yet our divorce rate soars, the marriage rate declines, and our ears ring with endlessly ticking biological clocks. Many of us edging 30 or past it fear that love will never be ours to have and hold. But why? Could it be that we are still seeking that one and only, the perfect mate? No? Well, listen to our songs.

Only you . . . no one but you . . . you alone . . . one alone . . . my one and only . . . I will wait for you, I'll never fall in love again, you are the only one, the perfect one for me, somewhere my love, you and you, all or nothing at all, exactly like you, never be another you, I only have eyes for you, very thought of you, you are my heart and soul, my sunshine, my lucky star, my everything . . . .

Maybe we haven't looked in the right places for it. After all, it is just around the corner, in April in Paris or Portugal, in blue Hawaii, in London and Atlantic City, in the chapel by the moonlight, on Moonlight Bay, in Manhattan, under the old apple tree, by the old mill stream, under Paris skies, somewhere in the night, day after day, only a moment, this magic moment, when we're dancin', in the spring, in the summertime, in the still of the night, by candlelight, by starlight, on the street and in the air, on New Year's, at Christmas, at Easter, when we wear a tulip, or as time goes by . . . .

We know what it is and should recognize it when it comes. It is what makes the world go round, something to live for, sweet and gentle, a taste of honey, a kiss to build a dream on, a kick, champagne, a wonderful day, a matter of time, young and foolish, a many-splendored thing, a tender trap, the sunniest day, a paper doll, a baby face, eyes of blue, eyes of green, eyes of brown, red sails, blue velvet, blue moon, a blinding flash, the wide wide world, what we fall in, build on, wait for a new kind of, what drives us crazy, what walks right in, what we're in the mood for, a habit, a funny Valentine, Joe, Billy, Cecilia, Stella, Julie, Caroline,

Maria, and Lisa Jane, moon, June, croon, tune and, of course—thanks to the Gershwins—blah, blah, blah . . . .

Come on—we all know love isn't perfect: the party's over, though everybody loves somebody, and we can't help lovin' still we're lonesome and blue, cryin' too, brokenhearted, don't get around much anymore, we beg them to say it isn't so, ask what they've done to our love, what now, because we're nobody till somebody loves us again. And that somebody, we know, will be perfect.

Well, we're here to tell you that *nobody* will be, but you *can* overcome your idealization of love and achieve a good and enduring relationship by achieving true understanding of your partner.

All Our Best Colors

Ah, Love, could you and I with Him conspire
To grasp this sorry scheme of things entire
Would we not shatter it to bits—and then
Remould it nearer to the heart's desire?
　　　　　—Omar Khayyám, *The Rubáiyát*

hy *can't* we find love? And why can't we keep it? After all, we think that we're informed, aware, and introspective. We know what love involves: tenderness, compassion, sensitivity, and sharing. So why is it so hard to attain?

The answer is simple. Love is all these things, but it's something else as well. It's knowing that *no person is made to meet the expectations of any other*. Genuine love, wrote Erich Fromm, means knowing that an individual is not an "object" of one's own desires but a separate being unto himself. Fromm meant to caution aspiring lovers against conceiving each other as the realization of a personal fantasy. The truth is this: there is no perfect person for you, and *you* cannot be a perfect person for someone else. We fail in love because all too often we forget this simple truth.

Chapter 1 described the ways in which we nurture an unrealistic image of a perfect other. Think now about how we try to make *ourselves* perfect in the eyes of another. When we meet someone new and think he or she may be "the one," we start, right away, to sail under false colors. We're on our best behavior and we often pretend to be what we are not. As the new person stops being so new and begins to know us, we let down our guard and relax our manner. And this is when the "love" may collapse. We not only don't have love, we don't have even a reasonable facsimile. We hasten to blame the other: He or she wasn't what we thought, didn't live up to our first impression, didn't go the distance well.

While it is true that the person may not have been what we imagined, it is also true that we have given a false impression. Both of us have been using "company" manners, not our true colors, not our best colors. We have constructed a facade. We have begun to play games, to embroider. To prevent this from happening again and again, it's time we exchanged the "eyes of love" for the "I's of love": our best colors, our second skin, an expression of our real and best self that we willingly and continually share with our loved ones. The I's of love are part of an ongoing action—not an act, not a staged performance—and they require labor and devotion.

These are the I's of love: INVOLVEMENT, INTERNALIZATION, and INTEGRITY.

1. *Involvement* means a willingness to explore and penetrate past the exterior physical being of the loved one into the interior landscape to the other's values, emotions, goals, and motivations.

2. *Internalization* means allowing the faculties of another person to become an integral part of our being and our world, and vice versa, with the desire to further the growth and development of both partners.

3. *Integrity* means honest interaction as well as preservation of the individuality of both partners in the relationship, not a merging and blurring into an indistinct mass.

If we add to the three I's the three R's of love—RESPECT, RESPONSIBILITY, and RECIPROCITY—we may achieve an enduring relationship.

1. *Respect*: The rule of respect demands that we cease considering the other a love "object." The love partner is neither an object nor a possession. Respect preserves both the true self and that of the other in the relationship. It establishes both partners in positions as guardians of the other's trust and confidence.

2. *Responsibility*: The rule of responsibility demands that immature love be left behind. It asks that feelings of manipulation, controlling, and exploitation be discarded. It assumes that love is conditional, and that rather than ask to be loved because we *are*, we ask to be loved for what we *can be*. Responsibility also implies that we are willing to continue the labor required to maintain a relationship.

3. *Reciprocity*: The rule of reciprocity implies mutual giving, not of material possessions, but of time, responsiveness, and loving consideration of the things the partner values in his or her person. Reciprocity also implies singularity. Let's face it: Time is limited and life is short. The act of love (not sex) takes a lot of time and labor.

Do you have the time? You betcha. Actually, you've probably spent more time and energy on improving your tennis, handball, gourmet cooking, or needlework than you have on improving your love relationships. And the reward of love is far greater than the rewards of such pastimes.

First , we ask you to examine yourself and the "Tender Me" that is within each of us, the delicate self that we don't expose easily to anyone, much less to the careless or the uncaring. In this Tender Me lives what you value in yourself and what you wish a partner to value, protect, and cherish. We ask you to decide what you believe you can offer another and continue to give unchanged without betraying your own Tender Me.

Then try to look past the physical being and manner of the new potential partner and make a rational choice. This isn't easy. When you first meet, you don't have much to go on. So go slow. Stop and reflect. And use only your best colors. Maybe you can learn to like wrestling and your partner will learn to love opera. It's worth trying. But if the interest isn't there, trot out your best colors and be honest. You don't have to have *all* the same interests.

Next, don't pretend. If warning signals are flashing before your eyes, take heed! Is that quick annoyance temper? Is that strict concern possessiveness? Explore your concern. If the answer to such questions is "yes," continue your search—with some one else.

Once you have reached your own definition of love, and what it is that you want to be loved and valued for, we ask you to do still more. We've dismissed "falling in love." Here we dismiss even Fromm's concept of "standing in love," an excellent concept of a continuing interchange of growth. What we ask you to practice is *understanding* in love. Love falters and dies from lack of this understanding—a word whose real meaning is not just communication (an imparting of facts or knowledge) but a true "standing among or under." When you understand your partner or let him or her understand you, there is no chance of lack of true communication, of misunderstanding. The best way to foster, achieve, and maintain understanding, we believe, is not a telephone call, not a tête-à-tête, but a LETTER.

Love Letters: A Little History

*They'll wish there was more, and that's the great
art o' letter-writin'.*
        —Charles Dickens, *Pickwick Papers*

hat *is* a love letter? That's what Linda wondered when she was ten and found in her aunt's attic a dusty brown paper bearing, in faint script, these words: "I think thee does not love me any more, Daniel. I haven't heard from thee in a day and a half." It was a letter from her great-grandmother Molly to her great-grandfather Daniel. It was one of a pile of letters tied together with faded ribbon.

In all, the letters, written in a four-year period during the Civil War, were a compelling private history set against the history of a nation. Daniel fought in the Union Army. Molly was a Southerner. Yet they were cousins. The letters told of a fourteen-year-old girl who risked her own safety to protect two "enemy" soldiers, bringing them food and nursing the one who was wounded.

They described the return of the two men to their own troops, detailed the sad state of those troops, and the deplorable conditions of Libby Prison, in which Daniel was held for two years. They described the harrowing journey of the girl and her brothers to Northern territory after the end of the war. They emphasized the devotion of two people whose love endured privation, separation, and the hostility that even today separates families whose members fought on opposite sides of that terrible conflict.

The letters ceased with the end of the war. Molly and Daniel no longer had need of letters. The rest of the details of their lives Linda learned from her father. Their lives were long, and the two parted only by death. But Linda's feelings of having known her great-grandparents stem from having read their letters. She was privileged to participate in their history. The letters of Molly and Daniel, not impassioned protestations of love, were a history of the daily intimate occurrences in two people's lives.

But that's just what love letters are—a history—a permanent record of the development of a relationship, a love, a life. Nothing else, no biography or autobiography, provides as telling a picture of people and their loved ones. The letter writer is not worrying about how she or he will be perceived by anyone other than the recipient of the letter. Thought and feeling are uncensored. And that is why the collected letters, particularly love letters, of the famous and infamous are so refreshing to read.

How else would we know of John Adams' longing to be with his wife Abigail and their children when, instead, he was laboring in the First Continental Congress: "Posterity! You will never know, how much it cost the present Generation, to preserve your Freedom! I hope you will make a good Use of it. If you do not, I shall repent in Heaven, that I ever took half the Pains to preserve it."

The birth pangs of our nation are delineated in a quarter-century's worth of correspondence between two people who were also the best of lovers and friends, as are the intimate and mundane details of their daily lives. Indeed, "dearest friend" is the term they most frequently used to address each other. We learn that John in his first throes of passion compared Abigail to the goddesses Aurora and Diana, that he was entranced by a "lady infinitely dear" and by the bright sparkle of her eyes, that her letters made his heart joyful, and that his to her were "more than gold and silver." The letters allow us to experience firsthand their pleasure in each other, their joy in the birth of children, their sorrows in illness and loss, their pangs of loneliness during long separation. They also tell of a love that endured long after physical beauty faded.

Leonard Wolff's letters to Virginia Stephen Wolff describe his passionate longing for her, the "perfect happiness" that the presence of this woman afforded him, she whose beauty took his breath away when he first saw her. Together with his letters to other friends, they give us a rich portrait of a devoted 25-year marriage of two great intellects, their works, both literary and social, and an intimate look at the activities of the Bloomsbury group. The letters also tell of Virginia's many long illnesses and the sacrifices Leonard's devotion required of him.

Napoleon's tempestuous letters to Josephine contained little other than passionate imploring that she join him, be waiting for him. She was his "absolute happiness" and her letters his only "balm." Yet they show that he was vulnerable, pardoning a man he had condemned to death because he was moved by the huge grief of the man's wife. They show a wildly jealous man who vowed to burst into Josephine's apartments to rend and tear the "new lover" he was convinced she had: "I detest you. Beware, Josephine, one fine night the doors will be broken down and there I shall be . . . ."

We have a greater understanding of a supposedly taciturn Woodrow Wilson when we read his first letters to Ellen Louise Axson, to whom he proposed after a brief courtship: "I am sick at heart from not hearing from you. It is now a week since you must have reached home and not a line have I heard from you." "Your sweet letters fill me with indescribable delight . . . I never knew what love was until I knew you." He progressed rapidly from great admiration for her good qualities to an intense passion, so great that even he was disturbed at its intensity. He is also revealed as jealous of the attentions paid to his fiancée by another man: "I do *not* believe in the possibility of [platonic love] *at all*. Of course, I have *perfect* faith in your discreetness." Yet he implored her to wear her engagement ring at all times.

Mark Twain's letters show him him as an intensely loving husband and father, "richer than any other person in the world," numbed with grief at the loss of first his daughter, then her mother: Now, " [I am] a pauper without peer . . . . Then we understood, and our hearts broke. How poor we are today. It is one of the mysteries of our nature that a man, all unprepared, can receive a thunder-stroke like that and live . . . . The mind has a dumb sense of vast loss—that is all." Samuel Clemens (Twain), who once determined that he "had been an author for 20 years and an ass for 55," was probably, and still is, America's greatest humorist, alternating between drollery and savage wit. Yet his letters reveal his profound capacity for love, his grievous loss of it.

The history of love letters is that they show all the sides of a relationship, the tragic and the comic, the domestic quiet and the sweep of passion. Entire lives are before our eyes.

Ancient Chinese poems are love letters. They illustrate lovers' quarrels: "With so much quarreling and so few kisses/How long do you think our love can last?" (Chin Dynasty). They tell of devotion: "How can I let you know of all my love? . . . When I think of all the things you have done for me,/How ashamed I am to have done so little for you . . . a poor return,/All I can give you is a description of my feelings" (Han Dynasty). The following ancient Egyptian lines describe the first thunderclap of love: "Ho, what she's done to me—that girl! And I'm to grin and just bear it? . . .

Dear god, give me relief." They describe the terrible plight of the lovesick (and its cure): "Let them call in the whole crew of specialists, my heart will not tick to their remedies . . . But if someone would say, 'There's a lady here waiting'—hear that, and you'd see me take heart in a hurry!" And these Egyptian lines foretell a lifetime: "Your love, dear man, is as lovely to me/As sweet soothing oil . . . As fragrance of incense . . . Like wine to the palate . . . While unhurried days come and go,/Let us turn to each other in quiet affection, walk in peace to the edge of old age. And I shall be with you each unhurried day."

More modern poets, such as Yehuda Amichai (Israel), tell of the power in love letters, which are not opened with a silver opener, but are "torn open, torn, torn" in the lover's desire to have "the sweetness of a letter between [his] eyes," even if if contains "a little blot . . . a tear that has melted ink." Chilean poet Pablo Neruda tells of love's endless evolution: "I love you in order to begin to love you/to start infinity again/and never to stop loving you." And even after death, when "there in the dust of my heart (where so many plentiful things will be stored),/You will come and go."

Linda has only sketchy memories of her grandparents and none of their letters. And if Linda's mother has any others than the small store she has revealed, she isn't telling yet. Linda says her own store is rather scanty—maybe 20 or 30 in all, some of them brief cards and tattered scraps with short notes. Among those she prizes most are those from her children, because children write shimmering, if brief, "love" letters. If we weren't journal keepers and "keepers" in general, we'd have few written remembrances of our loves and days.

Perhaps your store is scanty, too. Perhaps you, like so many others, pick card after printed card from a rack, hoping to find one that will tell another person your innermost thoughts and feelings. How much better told and more lasting your own history will be if you trust yourself to put in writing what no one else but you can say.

Eight Questions to Ask Yourself
Before Beginning

The cautious seldom err.
—Confucius, *The Wisdom of Confucius*

Ready? Set? Stop! It's time to ask yourself some questions:

1. To *whom* am I writing? Who is your recipient? Focus on your reader. The letter is intended for him or her. Imagine the reaction your letter will evoke. If your reader doesn't respond to poetry, don't write abstractly. You wouldn't give roses to someone who is allergic to flowers. Keep your reader foremost in mind as you write.

2. *What* is the *status* of this relationship, right now? Write a letter that is honestly appropriate to the present stage and status of your relationship. If you met last night, don't write an invitation to a getaway weekend. If you've just had your first date, don't

write a letter explaining what you need from a relationship. A love letter is not an exercise in dreaming. It's an exercise in genuine communication. Keep your eye on reality.

3. *What* am I writing? Are you writing what you really feel? You want your letter to contain your precise meaning. Be certain of your feelings before you begin. Express them with clarity and don't exaggerate.

4. *Why* am I writing? Communication and understanding are your aims. Manipulation sows the seeds for a failed relationship and has no place in love or a love letter. You are writing to express and explain yourself, to achieve better awareness of yourself and let your partner know you better. Your letters will strengthen and further your connection. They are a diary of your relationship's growth and development. Rereading them will allow you to relive their highlights and may help you over future stumbling blocks. Moreover, letters allow you time for reflection. Conversation is an act of immediacy and often an act of miscommunication, but you can write and rewrite a letter until you have written exactly what you want to say.

5. What do I want to achieve with *this letter* at *this time?* Stick to the point. Your letter is meant to elaborate your feelings and position right now. If you are telling someone how much you enjoyed your first date, you don't want to discuss what happened to your *last* relationship. If you are telling your partner you're sorry, you don't want to go over your unhappy childhood or all your previous disagreements.

6. *How* shall I write this letter? Maybe you never wrote a love letter in your life. No matter. What is most important about your letter is that it reflect you: your own feelings, genuine and sincere. It must also reflect the stage of your relationship. Make use of the checklists (the P.S.'s) in this book. You can also study and adapt the letters we've presented, but don't *copy* them word for word. That won't work. Your love letters must be just that—

your love letters.

7. *Should* I write this letter? Have you considered your situation carefully? Do you believe you perceive it and your partner fully and accurately? Does the letter suit the current dynamics of your relationship? What ramifications will your letter have? Remember too that you can't be certain that the response you get will be the response you seek. You are not writing a script with all the dialogue. You are writing only half a story.

8. Should I *mail* this letter? It's all down in black and white now. Once it's mailed, you can't get it back. Read this chapter again. Then decide.

AND MANY HAPPY RETURNS!

Letter to a Friend

Friendship is the breathing rose, with sweets in every fold.
—Oliver Wendell Holmes, "No Time Like the Old Time"

Yes' m, old friends is always best,
'lest you can catch a new one that's fit
to make an old one out of.
—Sarah Orne Jewett, *The Country of the Pointed Firs*

his feelings

"Friend" was once defined as someone who knows your faults but likes you anyway. Humorous, but too facile. A friend is a person you can trust without qualification and regardless of the circumstance. It's someone in whom you can confide your most intimate thoughts freely and without fear of betrayal. And friends confide back.

A friend will tell you the truth, even when you'd prefer not hearing it. Honesty is at the heart of every true friendship. A friend will give you careful, well-thought-out advice, but only when asked. Nor will a friend's nose get out of joint when that advice is ignored. Friends seek advice, too, and sometimes even follow it.

Friends remember your favorite colors and favored foods, your sizes, before and after when not to call, and the names of your other friends. They remember birthdays and anniversaries, too. Even silly ones like the first time you . . . but a friend would never tell.

A friend's a friend whether things are going well or poorly, whether you've got a buck or have just spent your last, whether you're in a good mood or are as sour as a lemon. Friends understand—that's what makes them friends. A friend watches your kids when you can't, laughs at the joke you've told before, splits the check or picks it up, assures you you'll get better, and includes you in when others include you out. A friend is the one who invites you over for Christmas dinner or the first Seder when you're alone. You do the same. Friends share.

A friend of the same sex never bird-dogs your date. A friend of the opposite sex helps you understand why their kind are frequently so difficult to get along with. And when an important relationship that you were counting on ends, friends are there to listen through the night. Friendship is a balm for broken hearts.

There are no age restrictions on friendship. Young with young, old with young, old with old: It works every which way. But same-age friends do seem to communicate just a bit more easily and, perhaps, as you get older you appreciate your remaining friends just a little more.

Friends have their own history, and that's a binding force greater than any super-glue. You need lots of acquaintances in life. You really only need one friend. If you took away absolutely everything I have—house, car, money, possessions, job—I'd still be a wealthy man if you left me my friend.

That's why I sometimes write my friend a love letter.

his Letter

Dear . . .

If that committee meeting had lasted another five minutes, I would have begun practicing my primal scream. The only good thing I can say about those monthly "bored" meetings is that you and I get to break bread afterwards and bring each other up-to-date on our lives.

Which, incidentally, gives me the opportunity to say "thanks." When I told you that I was in an up cycle lately, I neglected to add that you were responsible. I was getting too deeply involved with you-know-who. It was an imbalanced relationship and it hurt. You helped me put it into perspective. In a way, you fine-tuned my life and you did it so delicately. Everything is in much better focus now.

That's really the best thing about having such a close friend of the opposite sex. Suddenly there's someone to explain all those signals I've been missing for years!

No, that's not the best thing—not by far. The best thing is sharing and caring, having someone you can really count on. Each time we meet, we pick up our friendship just where we left off. There's no readjustment. After all this time, we know what to expect from one another. It's comforting, it's secure and, in a sometimes confusing world, it's important.

Or to put it more simply, I'm glad you're my friend.

Nyack, Sunday? C'mon up. Jeans, sweaters, and antiquing. It'll be fun—always is.

See you soon.

Sid

31

her feelings

What ever happened to Susan? Jamie? Can you recall your best friend in kindergarten, the girl or boy who shared your candy, your toys, your first hug or kiss, your first pledge of "friends forever"? What about your high-school friends, the ones with whom you shared sleepovers, giggles and confidences, the names of your secret crushes? Not a day went by when you didn't see each other, when you weren't ordered to "get off that phone right now!" You talked at school, at lunch, after school, and before bed—just one last thing you forgot to say.

What about your college roommate? You had all your classes together, discussed your dreams and goals, families, friends, and boyfriends, visited each other's homes, vowed you'd never lose touch with each other. And where are the friends of your early married life, the ones with whom you shared recipes, baby-sitting, pools, Brownie and Cub Scout duties, Little League and ballet lesson car-pooling? And coffee and lunches, dinners and movies, leisure with children spilling over your laps or rare moments snatched from the busy days and nights.

Do you sometimes remember the rare teacher whose sincere interest helped you to get through a tough subject or to make a decision about college and career? The elderly neighbor who showed you how to care for your roses or refinish the table that still gleams in the corner of your bedroom? Where is he now? Is he still living?

Many of us live far from our birthplaces or home towns. Families, jobs, and marriages take us far from our origins. We make new friends. In our busy lives, we have difficulty fitting even the new ones into our schedules. We send some of the old friends a card on holidays, maybe with a brief scribbled wish of our own added to the printed sentiment, maybe even a short note:

"We must see each other soon. I miss you." We mean it, too, but somehow another year slips by, the plans to meet or to write a real letter get lost in the crush of time.

Good friends are hard to come by, and all too easily lost if we don't keep up with what's happening in each other's lives. Greeting cards just aren't enough to accomplish this. And there's never "enough" time. You have to make the time. Why not write that special friend now?

her letter

Dear . . .

We see each other too seldom lately. We're both so busy.

I miss you. I miss the leisurely conversations we used to have. I miss the Saturday-night card games with your family, even though I always lost. I miss talking about our plans, our lives, the focus of our lives at that time: our children. Our youngest, our daughters. After all, they introduced us. From the minute they met when they were four years old, they were inseparable. Soon we were too. We had to be. They weren't allowed to cross the street alone, so we had to meet several times a day for the changing of the guard. It wasn't long before everything they had was inter-changeable: toys, clothes, beds, meals. If they didn't like the menu at one table, they simply presented themselves at the other. You won the two of them more often because you were a better and more imaginative cook. Each went happily off with the other family for an afternoon, a day, a weekend, as secure as though the parents were interchangeable too.

Funny how fast they've grown. They don't see each other much more often than we do, even though we all live so close. Yet their friendship endures.

I've never told you what having you for a friend has meant to me. You have been steadfast through all the ups and downs of my life. Yours was the company I sought when I was lonely and depressed during the rough times. Your genuine pleasure in sharing the good times enhanced my happiness. Yours was the first face I saw when I woke from anesthesia that time I was so ill. You were always first to offer words of comfort, as well as concrete help. You are the embodiment of a true friend. Having your friendship is an honor.

I have seen you help others in the same way. You are good, deeply loyal, worthy of trust. I have never heard you speak ill of anyone. You seem to see only the best in people. Somehow, maybe because of that, you always seem to have good people around you. Your daughters are good examples. They possess your same qualities.

I often think of the long, easy afternoons when our children were small, when we had time to talk, time to stroll the beaches as they played. How did the years slip by so fast?

I miss you. You are often in my thoughts. You will always be in my heart.

Love,
Linda

P.S | When you write your letter to a friend:

Do let your friend know *why* you value their friendship.

Do let your friend know how much their friendship means to you.

Do let your friend know that you want to return the friendship and can be counted on to do so.

Don't hesitate to express your genuine love to a genuine friend. How fortunate you are to have one.

Don't mix signals by hinting that you want something more in your relationship. That's another letter; it ain't this one.

C H A P T E R 6

When Friendship Turns to Love

The crown of these is ...
love and friendship, and sit high
Upon the forehead of humanity.

—John Keats, "Endymion"

his feelings

We had been friends for twenty months. The friendship had developed slowly, survived the usual misunderstandings, and deepened. Neither of us was in a hurry. We dated others with varying degrees of seriousness, shared confidences, supported each other when a problem arose at work or when, momentarily, health failed. There were shows and dinners on occasion, a gift here or there, a common cause in which we both became involved. We met each other's friends and family. We spoke on the telephone with increasing frequency. Gradually we opened up and began to discuss our longings, fears, hopes, and aspirations. We became each other's best friend. Whatever the uncertainties of life, we knew we could count on one another.

Our friends found our "relationship" a little strange. Truthfully, so did we. Harry had met Sally and they had stayed friends, nothing more. We used to say we loved each other but weren't "in love" with one another.

About this time, she broke up with a serious boyfriend. I knew it hurt though she handled it remarkably well. I was there for her as she had, in times past, been there for me. I think it was at this point that both of us began quietly comparing what we had with each other to what we thought we had with others. We began valuing our relationship differently.

Now when she called, I was just a little bit anxious, a little careful about what I said. When we were going to get together, I seemed to spend just a little more time picking out what shirt to wear, which tie. I thought of her more frequently and differently, and the thoughts lingered longer. Now when we spoke on the phone, there was a tinge of nervousness. It was as if, having known each other for almost two years, we were just beginning to date.

It was time to put my changing feelings on the line.

---

bis Lecter

Dearest . . .

I cannot be your friend anymore. At least, not just your friend.

Mind you, I think friendship is one of life's greatest joys, and I cherish ours. In my entire life I've never had a friend as close as you are to me. I know that "intimate" generally has another meaning, but we have truly been intimate with each other. We share everything: experiences, thoughts, feelings, and fears. You know more about me, about who I really am, than anyone ever has.

You praise my strengths and forgive my faults. I know, because you've told me so, that you feel the same way about us. We are each other's safe harbor.

But I cannot be your friend any more.

The past twenty months have been the most wonderful in my life. Knowing you, simply knowing you, has been the singular experience of my life. If nothing else good had ever happened to me, simply knowing you would still have made my life worthwhile. You are the most intuitive, compassionate, caring, tender, understanding person I have ever known. I must have done something very special in God's eyes for Him to have brought someone as special as you into my life.

Yet I cannot be your friend any more.

Nor can I tell you when I first knew. There was no particular moment, no lightning strike. Rather, a gradual awareness that we had become more than friends. Much, much more. That I was incomplete without you. That being with you brought me such happiness that being without you no longer made sense,

Something has changed. Still wine has become champagne. Friendship has become love. I do not know just when, but I do know why. You. You.

I cannot be just your friend. I am, I must be, more.

And because we have always been honest with each other, I thought you ought to know.

Sid

ḥER FEELIŊGS

Initial Comment:

1. "We were sure we were meant for each other the second we met. It was cymbals, bell, drums, and whistles. We couldn't get enough of each other."

2. "Instantaneous! We talked for hours and it wasn't enough. We ended up spending the next 36 hours together. We weren't apart for five hours for the next two months."

3. "I never met anyone like him before. Sparks flew. Flint and iron. We didn't see eye to eye on anything. It was so exciting."

4. "I don't know what she saw in me. But she sure pursued me. And what a turn-on!"

Three months later:

1. "Everything just dissolved. All physical, I guess. In three weeks, I found myself wanting to see other people—someone to talk with."

2. "It happened too fast, I guess. As long as we were alone, it was great, but when we got back to the real world, we were strangers."

3. "Not only didn't we see eye to eye, but in two months we were going at it tooth and nail."

4. "I don't know what I saw in her. I guess I liked what she seemed to see in me."

What a difference 90 days make. Sometimes it takes a lot longer. The crazy frenzy dissipates. The dream and the dream lover go up in smoke. What happened? Silly question. Answer: Fools rushed in. It's rare indeed that the immediate attraction that propels us into someone's arms or bed is real love. Real love grows slowly. You hear drums and cymbals? The orchestra is just tuning up. Bells and whistles? Watch out for the freight train. And hold on to your perspective.

Other comments:

"I'm not sure I'm in love. I haven't got that huge high. I feel comfortable. I'm never jealous or worried about where he might be."

"We're so relaxed together, whether we're reading the papers or out on the town. I can be myself with her."

"We always have something to talk about. We like being together but we like being by ourselves or with others, too. He's so easy to be with, but sometimes I think maybe we don't have enough electricity together."

What? No crashing chord? No torment of jealousy? No palpitations? How lucky they are. They are becoming good friends moving together toward love.

her Letter

Dear . . .

What a good friend you are. And what a good friend you have been for many years. Why I let you go that time we might have been more than friends I'll never know. But I did. What a shame. What better qualification could we have for being lovers than our enduring friendship?

That's why I feel so happy now—except when I think of the time I wasted. Your face makes me happy, the light in your eyes when you see me. Knowing that you are somewhere working, somewhere playing, just knowing you are somewhere makes me happy. In your arms, I feel at home, comfortable, warm and secure. I feel natural, completely myself and at ease.

When I read or hear of something interesting, I want to share it with you. That's because I know that you respond to many things in the same way I do. Predictable? No. I know that you will see other aspects as well and enlarge my feelings and reactions. I know it because of the books and knowledge you have shared with me in the past. The same things make us laugh, make us wonder, make us curious to know more.

I remember the times you were there as friend and confidante in the past, the kindnesses you showed me—freely—asking nothing in return. Even though you had many problems of your own, you gave me deep understanding and support whenever I needed it. So many of your friends and family, even your employees,

41

receive the same generosity of spirit from you. No wonder they love you. No wonder I do too.

You can cry, unashamed, because you have had much pain in your life. And it hasn't made you bitter or aloof. Quite the opposite, it has made you ever more sensitive to the pain of others, even more responsive. A gentle, loving man. A good man. A man of integrity.

You've got such a quick mind, so much creativity. Give the guy a #2 pencil and watch his smoke. And you're a little crazy, just like me. You see things just a tiny bit skewed, a little out of kilter. Just enough to know that money doesn't begin to be everything, that time for the soul is far more important.

Do you think I'll let you and love go away again? Not a chance! That crazy I'm not. But please, stay my friend forever.

Love always,
Linda

P.S. | When you write your "friendship turns to love" letter:

Do make sure your friend will welcome such a letter and not be confused by it.

Do take the time to explain the evolution of your feelings.

Do convey what you believe the change in your relationship will mean for both of you.

Don't let your letter be the first indication your friend has of the change in your feelings. It will be too sudden. All surprises are not necessarily welcome.

The "Blind Date" Letter: Responding to a Personals Ad

Look with favor upon a bold beginning.
—Vergil, *Georgics*, I

bis feelings

The paper pick-up seems to be the "in" way to meet people these days. "Personals" columns abound. Actually, nothing could be more impersonal. Yet, as we are caught between ever-increasing work pressures and ever-decreasing time to socialize, the magazine matchmaker seems to provide an efficient, if somewhat precarious, alternative. Safer than a singles bar, it's still a crap shoot. After all, truth in advertising laws don't apply here.

Let me tell you a true story. Last year, partially as an experiment and partially because a friend told me she had met someone special that way, I placed an ad in *New York Magazine*. The operative line was the tag, "What's more important, I never have a bad day." I got 435 responses! It got so I dreaded getting the mail. To this day, I occasionally find a photograph of some strange woman behind the sofa.

Through a series of evaluations, not all of which made sense, I winnowed them down to seven women whom I called and eventually dated. Ready? Of the seven, three had sent me photos of someone else! (Typical excuse: "I didn't have a current picture and that one looked so much like me." To whom?) Nevertheless, I did my best to make sure each of the women had a lovely evening and one I dated for a while.

Since then I felt it wiser to respond to such ads rather than place them. I've only done so five times, but I'm batting 1,000. All five chose my letter, among some others I'm sure, from a substantial response. They were five really nice women and I enjoyed getting to know them. Nothing serious developed, but that's the chance you take.

I kept one of the letters I sent and thought you might enjoy it. It may give you an idea or two. (And yes, I sent my *own* photograph—the one *without glasses*.)

ḥis Letter

Hi!

What a GREAT ad you wrote. Although I generally scan that column, mainly for the fun of it (everybody seems so "perfect"), I never thought I'd write a reply. But there was just something about your ad that was so creative, engaging, and genuine that I really wanted to meet the person behind it.

Now, please don't tell me that your brother wrote the ad and that I'm going to have to take him to dinner at "One if by land..." (Been there? It's in the Village, has a fireplace, a wonderful pianist, and flowers everywhere. So romantic!)

The essayist E.B. White wrote: "He who sets pen to paper writes of himself whether knowingly or not." Brief though your ad was, I think it told me some important things about you: You clearly have a sense of style, you lead an active life, and you have a super sense of humor. Have you any idea how long I've been waiting for you?

As for me, I fit your mathematical requirements (age, height), your educational and professional ones (ivy, lawyer), and we share almost all the same interests (travel, theater, tennis: Yeah! Do you mind terribly going to the ballet yourself? Okay, okay, I'll learn to plié, but will I look silly in a tutu!). Oh, I play piano—not important stuff, just light jazz (helped get me through school.) And yes, I'm also looking for the "right one."

But first comes friendship.

No . . . . First comes a quiet dinner at "One if by land."

I'm enclosing a business card and I've written my home phone number on it. Who knows, maybe you know someone who needs a good lawyer.

Failing all that, how about writing an ad for me? Preferably one that will get me a date with someone just like you.

Call soon . . . sooner . . . soonest.

Sid

her feelings

When you answer a personal ad you know you're writing to someone who's searching for a partner and you know to some extent what kind of partner he wants. If you select the right ad, and in response compose the right letter—you just might meet a friend, a companion, even a lover.

Among the hundreds of personal ads you might find in a single magazine, two or three might really offer you the chance for a relationship. Your job is to eliminate systematically those that won't. Give the ads a first reading and ignore everything the men say about themselves. Pay attention, instead, to what they say they *want* from a partner. Eliminate immediately those who focus primarily on the physical. Guys who are looking for "a perfect 10," a "knockout," "a satin and lace type," or "great legs and body to match" are not interested in having a relationship, even if they think they are. You might actually be a "knockout" or a "perfect 10," but why waste your time on a guy who values these qualities above all others. Also eliminate men who say they're "free in the afternoons" or "in town every other weekend." These guys are married and they're not looking for love.

Okay. Your list is getting smaller. Among the guys who remain, toss out the ones who "have it all." If he says he's handsome, sensitive, and a self-made millionaire, you ought to wonder why he's alone. Either he isn't all he claims to be or there may be a little more to his story than he's telling. Maybe he's also a pathological liar or will be reporting to his probation officer for five more years.

Your list is smaller still. Now look for someone with whom you can *do* something. If you like sailing, find a sailor. If you like poetry readings, find a writer. We all know that shared interests do not guarantee love. But meeting someone for the first time can be a lot easier if you meet for a mutually enjoyed activity instead of a drink or a cup of coffee.

Now, you've chosen your ad—or two or three. Before you write, remember three things: First, see the letter for what it is—an attempt at meeting someone new, not a full-blown love letter. Second, be casual. Write as though you were talking to someone you'd just met at a party or other social event. And you *haven't* met. So why talk, as some people do in their ads, about commitment and the "M" word? Third, be honest. If his ad is honest and your answer is too, you may have a great thing going.

A friend of mine answered the following ad:

"Tell me about yourself: your life, work, favorite things—music, books, sports. I'm a so-so artist, employed as a writer, love concerts in the park, hotdogs on the beach, and skiing. I'm a book lover, animal lover, and an indoor botanist. Would love some company in my pursuits. I'm average height, brown hair, blue eyes, 40-ish, and divorced. If you're a woman who would like to share these and other interests with me, please respond. Age, race, religion unimportant. Phone number and brief description would be nice. AOX1342."

She answered as follows:

ÞER LETTER

Dear AOX1342,

This is a little awkward, writing into space, so I'll get the awkward part over with. If I were before you, you'd see a slender woman with dark hair and eyes. I don't know your criteria for attractiveness, but I feel fairly comfortable with mine.

My life is a bit hectic, since I work for myself and I have to be a pretty tough boss or the employee would always be out to lunch. Still I'm not a 9-to-5-er and can be a little free of the clock.

Why am I writing to you? Well, I'm single too. It's hard enough to meet people who share your interests and it's harder when you work alone. Your ad made me feel we might have enough things in common that we would enjoy spending some time together. I love books. Some of my best time off is spent in a library or bookstore, not looking for any book in particular, just browsing. I also love to paint (watercolor), but Christie's and Sotheby's aren't beating down my doors yet.

My favorite music? Well, it's eclectic. I like Teddy Wilson and Roy Orbison. Linda Ronstadt, Roberta Flack, and Kiri Te Kanewa. John Renbourne and Luciano Pavarotti.

My favorite book? Too many to count. But you might consider The Last of the Just *by André Schwartz-Bart or* The Once and Future King *by T.H. White. My favorite sport? Skating—but I'd like to have a skier show me the slopes.*

You say you're an indoor botanist. I have a house and love to stroll my "south 40." All 5,000 square feet of it to check its growth, or what's left of it by August. It's always way ahead of my efforts by then.

Does all this mean we may hit it off? Who knows? I'd like to meet you for a walk on the beach or a trip to the zoo or your favorite book store. You can reach me at XIX-3477.

Looking forward to hearing from you,

. . .

P.S. | When you respond to a personals ad:

Do read the ad again. This time look for the traits or interests that might be a turn-off. Why start something you may be unwilling to finish?

Do tell enough about yourself so the recipient can make an informed decision about whether to call you.

Do use a little humor. Everyone appreciates a good laugh and it's a sign of mental health.

Don't lie. First it's immoral and second, you'll be discovered eventually. (Or, first you'll be discovered eventually and . . .)

Don't engage in overkill. This is your letter, not your biography.

Don't appear desperate. Who needs a loser?

Don't send someone else's picture unless you intend to see each other only at masquerade parties.

Don't sell past the close.

We Met Last Night

Some enchanted evening . . .
—Oscar Hammerstein II, *South Pacific*

Love conquers all things; let us surrender to Love.
—Vergil, *Eclogues*

ḥis ḟeeLiṇgs

They met at a party and he took her home. Next day he called to see if she was free to join him for dinner that evening. She agreed and was pleased by his spontaneity. He hadn't waited the "required" three days before calling, nor had he asked her out for "sometime next week." He obviously wasn't into games. Straightforward and direct, that was his style, and it suited her just fine.

Under those circumstances, I much approve. It was a singles party, she let him take her home, and she had given him her telephone number. He had indications both that she was available and that his attention would be welcome. But the situation isn't always so clear-cut.

The circumstances of your initial meeting may have prevented you from spending much time together. You may not have obtained a phone number or it may be unlisted. Although you know the person is not married, you may be unaware of their social situation or the current state of their other involvements. It may simply be that you were attracted or entranced, but from a distance. You may not have had the opportunity to "sell" yourself, even a little. There are many reasons why a phone call follow-up may be just a little bit too direct. A brief informal letter such as the first that follows can serve as an ice-breaker, a predicate to your subsequent call. It can be a gracious gesture and a surprisingly welcome one. Some of my happiest relationships have begun that way. The second letter is a bit of whimsy for those who enjoy a game now and then and are willing to let the other person play, too. I used it once some years ago when I didn't know much about her, especially whether she'd be at all receptive. She loved the letter and we played together for more than a year. Nobody won and nobody lost, but we enjoyed the game.

his Letter

Dear . . .

Meeting you was clearly the highlight of last evening's event. I am in our host's debt.

Although we did not get to spend much time together, it was enough for me to know that I'd like to see you again. Putting aside (although why, I do not know) that I found you charming and charismatic, we obviously have several interests in common. Moreover, I found what you had to say both interesting and insightful and hope you will expand upon it over lunch or dinner soon.

I'll be away on business until the early part of next week and will call you then to see if you are free.

I certainly hope so.

Sid

ANOTHER OF HIS LETTERS

Dear . . .

You have been selected to participate in a dating preference survey by _____, who met you last night at _____. This survey is to be completed in its entirety and returned in the enclosed, self-addressed envelope in time for all arrangements to be made, reservations secured, and tickets obtained, but in no event later than _____. Thank you for your participation in this completely random and anonymous market research project.

1. I prefer being called for:
  A. _____ At my home.
  B. _____ At my office. (Address: _____

_____)
  C. _____ Neither. I prefer meeting at the restaurant, theater, or event.
  D. _____ Neither. I will meet you at your home or office. (Circle one. Here are my addresses: _____

_____)
  E. _____ At my boyfriend's house. (If this item is checked, it will not be necessary to complete the rest of the survey.)
2. I will be ready:

    A. _____ at 6:30 p.m.

    B. _____ at 7:00 p.m.

    C. _____ at 8:00 p.m.

    D. _____ I am always ready.

3. On a date, I like to: (Check all that apply.)

    A. _____ See a movie, a show, a concert, a ball game, the opera, the ballet. (Circle one.)

    B. _____ Enjoy a quiet dinner.

    C. _____ Go dancing.

    D. _____ Make out.

4. My favorite food is:

    A. _____ Continental.

    B. _____ Oriental.

    C. _____ Seafood.

    D. _____ Big Mac, fries, and Coke.

5. I prefer dining:

    A. _____ Before.

    B. _____ After.

    C. _____ During.

6. My favorite listening music is :

    A. _____ Classical.

    B. _____ Jazz.

    C. _____ Country and Western

    D. _____ R & B, Rock 'n Roll, Heavy Metal (Circle one.)

    E. _____ Lullabies.

7. I like to dance to:

    A. _____ Big bands

    B. _____ Disco.

    C. _____ Lambada (please!)

    D. _____ Folk dancing.

    E. _____ Break dancing.

8. I smoke:

A. _____ *Always.*

B. _____ *Never.*

C. _____ *Only when I'm dry and on fire.*

9. *To me, the word "dutch":*

A. _____ *Is anathema.*

B. _____ *Means to share costs.*

C. _____ *Refers to someone from the Netherlands.*

10. *On a first date, I always:*

A. _____ *Dress to kill.*

B. _____ *Discuss the colors I'd like for my wedding.*

C. _____ *Talk about daddy.*

D. _____ *Bring mad money/business cards/ condoms (Circle all that apply.)*

E. _____ *Invite my date up for a nightcap and what-have-you.*

11. *On a first date, I never:*

A. _____ *Hold hands.*

B. _____ *Talk about my other relationships.*

C. _____ *Promise more than I'm willing to deliver.*

D. _____ *Invite my date up for a nightcap and what-have-you.*

12. *For statistical purposes only, please provide the following information (optional):*

I am:

_____ *Single.*

_____ *Involved.*

_____ *Married.*

_____ *Separated.*

_____ *Divorced.*

_____ *Confused.*

In appreciation for your cooperation in completing this survey, our representative will call you in the very near future to suggest a custom-tailored date based on the information you have supplied.

her feelings

You were introduced at an art gallery opening, at a friend's home, at a party. Or you met him at a dance, on the beach, at work, during a vacation. Or you met him at a class reunion. He's brand new but you feel as though you've known him forever. He's witty and knowledgeable about politics and art. Wonderful! A sense of humor is high on your list of desirable qualities, you are active in local politics, and a painter. Or you knew him in high school and boy how he's changed! Five inches taller, twenty pounds heavier (and every ounce of it attractive), and thoroughly at ease with himself. And with you.

Once you met, no matter how you met, you couldn't see anyone else in the room. He didn't seem to either. He didn't leave your side all evening. You continued your sparkling conversation over sparkling wine late into the evening at a nearby café. You exchanged phone numbers.

Now it's morning, the cold light of day. It wasn't just the lights, the wine, or the music. You still find just the thought of him exciting. In retrospect, the night is still perfect. You want to tell him so. And you can't wait for his call. You don't have to.

Write him a note. Don't go overboard. Don't come on like gangbusters. You *like* him. Don't pick out your wedding gown and your children's names. But no matter how excited you feel, you're not in love—yet. Tell him you enjoyed meeting him. Tell him you enjoyed his company. Tell him he made an otherwise unremarkable event memorable. Who knows what will happen next?

her Letter

Dear . . .

Just think! I was going to stay home and clean out my closets last night. Even cleaning closets seemed preferable to going to another opening. Am I glad I didn't. Do you realize that was the first time you ever saw me without a mouthful of wire? How I used to hate it when the kids called me "metal mouth." You never did. Anyway, the wires did their job. I can hold a straw with my bottom lip these days.

I'm glad I changed my mind last night for two reasons. First, I saw you again. And what a welcome sight you were. I don't think I knew one other person there. Second, the show was great, diverse and original.

There's a third reason, actually. I had a wonderful time with you, at the show and afterwards, catching up on past and present. I'd like to catch up some more. How would you like to meet me at the gallery Saturday afternoon so we can see the show at leisure? It was so crowded that I didn't get a chance to walk through again. You have my number. Let's be in touch soon.

Linda

P.S. When you write to the person you met last night:

Do note where you met. It may have been a long night.

Do remind the recipient who you were. It's just possible you are slightly less memorable than you think.

Do say why you want to get to know the person better —what it was that attracted you.

Do keep it light.

Do leave room for the possibility the recipient is already involved.

Don't come on too strong. None of this, "I met you last night and already I'm in love with you." This is an invitation not a proposal.

Letter to an Old Flame: "Do You Remember When . . . ?"

For what thou lovest well remains, the rest is dross,
What thou lov'st well shall not be reft from thee.
—Ezra Pound, "Contra Naturam"

his feelings

We are the sum total of all our experiences. The more intense the experience, the more it affects and shapes us. Since few experiences are as intense as our romantic ones, our personalities are in large part shaped by those we have loved. In such a way do they remain part of us forever.

No one who has loved and lost is ever completely "over it." Rather, we are all a little bit like the Roman god Janus, who had two faces—one looking backward and one forward. Although it is unwise to live in the past, it is important to come to terms with it. Only by resolving past conflicts can we hope to avoid future ones and move on with our lives.

Since each person I have loved has become part of who I am, I could no more forget them than I could forget my right arm. Nor would I want to. Each of them was so important to me and, with the rarest exception, such a grand person that I cherish the memories of the time we shared. They were a significant part of the sweetness of my life.

Of course, I do not keep in touch with all of them. In some cases, we have lost track of one another; in others, doing so might disrupt present lives and would therefore be inappropriate. But I do keep in touch with a few "old flames." I might do so once, in any case, just to help me understand the "break-up" and put it behind me. (Or to help them understand, as the case may be.) Otherwise it is difficult to close the door. In other instances, we have simply become friends and, having shared part of each other's past, we enjoy sharing part of each other's present.

In one instance, together and apart, we have shared each other's life for more than a decade. I loved her so much that the word "love," as powerful as it is, seems insufficient to describe the feeling. But sometimes love isn't enough. It was, I think, a matter of bad (or at least unfortunate) timing. If we met today and weren't "involved" with others, I believe it would work beautifully. But one deals with what one is given. What was, was. What we enjoy now are the glowing embers of memories that warm us whenever we need warmth.

On occasion, we fan those embers with a letter.

his Letter

Dearest . . .

The colors, oh the colors! Fiery reds and oranges, magenta and the deepest purple, blues of every hue, hints of mauve, wisps of white.

I am sitting atop "our" retaining wall behind the Pioneer Inn watching the setting sun struggle against the great god Maui's lasso. Mama's tapa cloth will be good and dry tonight,

This spot, this one spot in all the world, is my "happy place." Eat your heart out, B'rer Rabbit!

Do your remember when. . .? I seem to ask you that so frequently, yet never more so than when I return to Kamehameha's kingdom. Each stream overflows, each crevice is filled, with memories of the times we spent here. And that, of course, is why I keep coming back—to recapture, if but for a moment, something of what we shared here. Were ever two people as happy?

I have, after all, watched the sunset over the Gulf of Finland during the White Nights, over Jerusalem the Gold, and across West Lake in Hanchow as the mist rose from a thousand lotus leaves. All exquisite. All memorable. Why should the sunset here always appear more beautiful to me? Because this was our sunset. Here we watched hand-in-hand as the sun slipped ever so slowly beneath the horizon. Here our grips tightened as we bid it goodnight. Here we embraced and departed in silence. It was our secret, sacred ritual.

The beaches here bear our initials from a thousand hearts drawn in the sand. The trade winds rustling through the cane murmur the private names we reserved for each other. Each flower's perfume reminds me of you. No wonder I return. No wonder I write you each time I do.

It is almost dark. Only the lights of Lahaina make it possible *for me to see the distant shore. The moon has not yet made its entrance and soon both Lanai and the sun will fade from view.*

I miss you, but more, I remember you. For the things you taught me, for the joy you brought me, and for the memories you left me, I will always be grateful. And if I am saddened by the darkness that has now enveloped me, I am comforted by the sure knowledge that the sun also rises.

Sid

more of his thoughts

We lived across the street from each other. She was my sweetheart during my senior year in Forest Hills High School and my freshman year at Columbia. It was the Fifties, a time of innocence, a lovely time. Although our romance ended and I lost touch with her, over the years I thought of her often. I remembered her as the most beautiful girl I'd ever known. "Gorgeous" just began to describe her. In fact, she subsequently went on to become a beauty contest winner and into an aspect of motion picture production.

But her beauty was only one reason she stuck in my mind. She had a certain quality about her, a magnetism that set her apart. Possessed of a super satirical sense of humor, she was also gentle, candid, loving and kind. The word hadn't developed its own currency then, but she definitely had an "aura"—a sort of star quality.

A very few days ago, after more than thirty years, she saw me crossing the street with a business colleague. She waited until I went into a bank, approached the colleague to ascertain my identity, presented her business card and disappeared. When, a few moments later, the card was given to me with her maiden name written on it (she had married and divorced as had I), I was stunned, confused, and elated.

An exchange of phone calls ensued and we arranged to meet

for lunch at the Jockey Club. The moment she entered I recognized her. Despite the years she had retained her great beauty. Now, however, to that beauty was added an elegance, a stature, a regal demeanor. She was truly a work of art. We embraced instantly and it was as if we were once again at her doorstep in Kew Gardens Hills kissing goodnight on her front porch.

During lunch I had a dozen long-stem roses delivered to her. The next day helium balloons were sent to her home announcing our "anniversary," for we were now "one day old." The next evening she met me at the ballet.

The situation isn't without complications. It rarely is. She's away on a trip right now which gives us both time to think about what has happened to us. I've done my thinking. It's time to write to my old flame.

ANOTHER OF HIS LETTERS

My darling . . .

I am sitting in the den. The house is still. It is so late I fear to look at the clock. My head is filled with the beautiful strains of "Swan Lake." My heart is filled with you.

These past few days have been wonderful. You appeared out of nowhere, this elegant "princess" from my past, and changed my whole life. It has been a decade since I remember feeling so alive, so happy, so hopeful.

We are a miracle, you and I. A miracle. We bear witness to three truths I want to shout from the rooftops, share with the world:

> *"In your heart you never grow old."*
> *"You're never too old to be in love."*
> *"Love really can last a lifetime."*

"In your heart you never grow old." The moment we saw each other, I was 19 again and you were 16. Holding you in my arms, we were once again coming home from the Main Street movies or a school dance, saying our tender goodnights in the shadows of your front porch. We trembled, we were gentle—just the way we were then. We were fresh and new and young again. We and the world were alive once more!

"You're never too old to be in love." We held hands throughout our lunch and two nights later throughout the ballet. It was as if we were afraid to let go for fear we'd lose each other again. The maître d' said it made his heart happy to see us so engrossed in one another despite the fact that dish after dish was removed untouched. We were thirsty—not for the wine but for each other. And the taste of your lips was all I needed to end the hunger in my heart.

"Love really can last a lifetime." Our own personal histories had made us doubt that. But now we knew that a part of each of our hearts had always been reserved for the other. Even as we rushed to bring each other up to date on our pasts, we talked about the future and what it would be like together. The love was so clearly there. Only the logistics needed to be worked out. Having found each other, after more than 30 years, could we let anything stand in our way?

I am old enough to know that one can't predict the future. Man plans and God laughs. But how I pray we will weave our lives together for that fabric will truly be indestructible.

You talked of dreams that had not come true. There is still time! You talked of aspirations unfulfilled. There is still time!

You talked of plans long since abandoned. There is still time! Herzl said, "If you will it, it is no dream." All the things you wanted can still be yours. All the love that has been lacking is waiting for you in my arms. I have loved you all my life. I love you still. Whatever days are left are yours. The only goal I have remaining is your happiness. You have given me back my youth.

Sid

ђER ϝEELIЛGS

It's rare that we have only one love in our lifetime. Sometimes we slip past a special love. Childhood sweethearts go off to separate colleges. Lovers are separated geographically, and with time and distance, encounter new and stronger love. We find that we are too diverse. Old interests and goals have faded, and we find partners who share our new ones. Sometimes, timing just isn't right: it's too soon and we're not ready to be involved for a lifetime.

But the old flame comes to mind suddenly when we find a poem or card among old papers, when we hear a fragment of song that was "our song." We have an eerie sense of déjà vu when we find ourselves in a place that was "our place" or see a face, a walk, a gesture that reminds us of our past love. The memories are pleasant, and we stir the embers happily, and we wonder if they remember us as fondly as we remember them.

You may want to contact an old flame. You may not be involved with anyone, know that he isn't either, and hope to renew a past relationship. Great. I hope it works. Some embers, though, are better left alone. Don't stir them up with a letter, if (1) you may be interfering with someone's new life and love, (2) you're feeling nothing more than boredom or nostalgia (you may be inviting a renewal of a relationship you really have no wish to pursue), (3) you're angry with your present lover and you're trying to stir up more than old embers (you might end up with two old flames).

Sometimes you may want to write a letter to an old flame just to understand what went wrong, to say things you never got a chance to say, to understand your part in the relationship. It can be a revealing and satisfactory experience. And you don't have to mail it.

ḣer Leꞇꞇer

Dear . . .

You've stayed a part of my life all this time even though I haven't seen you for three years. So many things remind me of you. Some Irish song, a certain face.

Do you remember when I kidnapped you from 10th Street and took you to the "wilds" of Orient Point? Do you remember our walk out on the point, that tiny strip of land with water converging on us from both sides? The smooth "egg" stones—some so perfect that they seemed to be fooling the gulls into hatching them? At least we persuaded ourselves that's what was happening.

Do you ever think of Mitchell's? The old one, that is. Our room there with the tin shower? Every time we showered, it sounded like a revolution was taking place.

I think about it. I remember sprawling on the dock at midnight while you pointed out constellations: the Pleiades, Cassiopeia. The stars were so bright without all the backlight of the city.

I remember you laughing, outlined against the sun—laughing at me gathering rocks, telling me I needed those rocks in my pocket to keep the wind from blowing me away. I remember you in the dining room at Mitchell's, showing me how to coax reluctant snails from their shells. I remember the startled diner at the next table who suddenly had snail soup.

I remember you in the bar, more than a little smashed on Black Russians, tap dancing up and down the short flight of stairs to the dining room, imitating James Cagney, singing, breathless.

I remember you in Brighton, at Coney, eating hot dogs at Nathan's, in Garrison, in Saranac, at the Cedar and the No-Name, at Emilio's, and on Great Jones Street. I remember you in *success and elation, in failure and anguish. With great pleasure and with pain.*

And by the way, where are you tonight? And do you remember me?

Love,
Linda

P.S. | When you write to your old flame:

Do let the reader know why they are remembered fondly.

Do place that relationship in the context of the rest of your life and develop the theme of its meaning to you.

Do bring to mind specific significant events in your relationship.

Do note how often you think of her or him.

Do leave room for the possibility the recipient is involved with another.

Don't expect too much. We do not all view the past the same.

Don't expect the person you are writing to not to have changed over the years. We all change.

Letter to a Former Spouse

*Marriage resembles a pair of shears, so joined that they
cannot be separated; often moving in opposite directions,
yet always punishing anyone who comes between them.*
    —Sydney Smith, *Lady Holland's Memoir*

ḣis ꝼeeliꞃgs

O nce you love someone, a part of your heart always
belongs to them. No matter how wrenching the final
parting, time passes and heals, memories fade. Ultimately,
it is indeed the laughter that we remember.

Long relationships in particular develop a "history" of their
own, and that history does not evaporate when the relationship
ends. Nor do the feelings which sustained it. They survive in the
hidden recesses of our hearts. One day, when you least expect it,
it all comes back to you with as great intensity as before—why you

fell in love in the first place.

But why write a love letter to an "ex"? There are many reasons: perhaps because you are interested in reconciliation, or in maintaining a good relationship for the family's sake, or in keeping alimony demands down or payments up.

It's useless to harbor bad feelings. Better to leave them in the vault with the final papers. With so many marriages ending in divorce and with so many children affected, how much more constructive to keep only the good memories alive and to express them every so often.

I have written to my former spouse on occasion. No one who knows us would be surprised. Why, we have even been asked to run PTA programs on "successful divorce." Suffice it to say, she's one of my best friends and I am grateful to have had her love for as long as I did.

And sometimes I like to tell her so.

his Letter

Dearest . . .

You were right about one thing (about a lot more than one thing). I'll "never learn."

Earlier today, while reaching up in the hall closet to get some tennis balls (Use a step stool? Nah, I'm tall enough!), I knocked over one of the photo albums. You've heard, I suppose, of the "domino effect"? Years of pictures tumbled down like leaves in Autumn. Thus did I spend the afternoon reinserting and reminiscing.

Now I know why you became such a beautiful woman. Lord, were you a gorgeous girl! I look at the photographs of you on campus and it's clear why I was considered the luckiest guy at school. Then there are those pictures of our early days in Ro-

chester. I'd forgotten there was that much snow in the entire world. And the shots of the kids at Christmas; those are my favorites. (Do you remember the nights we spent trying to assemble the toys? We spent hours just trying to find the elusive "Tab C" to stick into "Slot A.")

The clambakes in Maine, the big trip to Disneyland, the graduations and confirmations, the pictures of some of our relative who now live with God—all there.

It was a life and I treasure the life that it was. Sure there were some really rough spots, no hiding that. But when I see what a fine job you've done with our daughter—and when you compliment me on how our son has turned out—why we didn't do so badly after all.

So on this day spent looking back, I thought I'd just drop you a note to say that with all the ups and downs, I'd rather have had you for my wife for all the years we were together than anyone else in the world.

Someday we'll see the kids married and there will be grand-children. There is much good yet ahead of us and it comes from the good we had in us.

And it's the good that I remember, whenever I remember, the way we were.

Sid

P.S. | When you write to your former spouse:

Do recall the good times.

Do let your spouse know that in the time that's passed you have learned to appreciate him or her anew.

Do praise their strengths and virtues.

71

Do say you're sorry for whatever wrong things you may have done.

Don't dredge up yesterday's dirt.

Don't say hurtful things—better not to write.

Don't ask for something. A request should be a direct request, not camouflaged as a loving letter.

After the First Date

Getting to know you, getting to know all about you . . .
—Oscar Hammerstein II, *The King and I*

his feelings

We were sitting in a coffee shop discussing her new relationship. He was particularly thoughtful, she explained, and proceeded to prove it with a charming story:

They had met through a personals ad. Their first date was for cocktails at a quaint cafe downtown. She really liked him and thought it had gone well. But she had been disappointed before when, on occasion, someone she liked hadn't called again. So as she took the subway back home, she was just a bit anxious.

As she entered her apartment, her answering machine light was flashing. He had timed his call to ensure that his message would be there when she arrived. He wanted her to know that he thought she was "pretty special" and hoped they'd see each other again soon. (They've been together two years now and, unless I miss my guess, those are wedding bells you hear in the distance.)

A nice touch—letting the person you have just dated for the first time know you enjoyed the evening and plan to call again. Those first impressions we give and receive are extremely important. As any trial lawyer knows, jurors tend to make up their minds after opening statements and it is very difficult to get them to change later on. If ever being thoughtful, considerate, and communicative count, they count early in the relationship.

You don't want to overdo it, of course. If you come on too strong, you are likely to scare the other person away. (Ouch, have I been guilty of that!) There's a line to draw, but you needn't be Rembrandt to draw it.

Last Sunday, I had an absolutely delightful first date. We went to an annual event called "A View from the Vineyards." It's a tastings party sponsored by California wineries and is catered by several different restaurants. It's always a fun evening, but she made it more so. She was wonderful company: relaxed, engaging, vivacious. The letter you are about to read I am actually writing to send to her. Wish me luck!

his Letter

Dear . . .

From the moment I called for you last Sunday, I knew it was going to be a great evening—and was it ever!

You looked terrific, simply terrific. (I loved your reply when I told you so. "Thanks. But what did you expect?") I don't know what I expected, probably had no expectations, but that yellow and black outfit looked sensational. Or more accurate, looked sensational on you.

More important, you were positively effervescent. Yes, the party was exciting and so very different—roaming from room to room tasting all those wines and sampling the various hors-d'oeuvres. (Thank heaven for the hors-d'oeuvres or we'd never have gotten home. Home? We'd never have found the car!) And what a surprise it was to run into folks from your home town. Unexpected reunions are the best. But I've been to super parties before. It wasn't the party. It was clearly you who made the evening special.

So much laughter, such great conversation! I really enjoyed talking to you but not half as much as I enjoyed listening to you. You are one of the most interesting, open, and insightful people I've ever met. There were times when, surrounded by others, I was oblivious to anyone there but you.

You describe yourself as being an "upfront person." I admire that and hope to emulate it. Let me tell you, then, that I had more fun last Sunday evening than I can remember having had in much too long. I know you have both an active professional and social life but trust you'll find a way to make some time for us. I surely will—because I want to see you again.

There are worse things to have than fun—and worse things to be than happy.

I'll call soon.

Sid

her feelings

Do you tremble when you have a first date? Is the trembling excitement or anxiety? It may be the latter. When we meet others for the first time or under new circumstances, we want to make a good impression. We want others to like us, to find us interesting.

We're opening ourselves to new prospects and exploring unknown territory. It's natural to feel a little anxiety. When you date
for the first time, even if you're an old hand at dating and even if
your date is not a blind date but someone you've already met, your
anxiety level can increase. The first date can be awkward. You've
upped the stakes past mere social interaction. You are investigating
the possibility of a love relationship. You're on new ground and
you're on a voyage of discovery.

You may not experience any awkwardness. Lucky two. You
hit it off from the beginning. The unknown territory seems
familiar and comfortable. You share a concert or a dinner and
discover common tastes in music or food. Your conversation
discloses other mutual likes and dislikes. You both love *Taxi* and
The Odd Couple, mystery stories. You both dislike spectator
sports. You have a wonderful time and neither of you seems to
want it to end. He asks to see you again and you are delighted. So
much for anxiety. Evidently you've made a good first impression
on each other. No question. First impressions are important. So
are seconds. That's why it's important to let your date know that
you enjoyed his company and your time together. Write and tell
him so.

ÞER LETTER

Dear . . .

*Thanks for one of the best evenings I've had in a long time. I
enjoyed the show so much. You either have magic powers or you
planned this for a long time. I've wanted to see it for six months
and I'd heard it was sold out for six months more.*

*Dinner was delightful too. You've spoiled me thoroughly. My
lunch today is my standard—Swiss cheese, lettuce, and tomato on
a roll. Nonetheless, candles seem to be flickering on my desk, and*

I can hear music.

You're so easy to be with. I was so engrossed in the show that you must have thought I was mute. I made up for it at dinner. You barely got a word in edgewise. It's your fault. You got me started on my favorite author. I must say you have good taste. You like the same books I do, and the same desserts.

How do you feel about Swiss cheese? Or won-ton? Or pizza? Pick the menu that suits you and it will be on the table at 8:00 Friday. With some wine, but one of a little more recent vintage than the one we shared last night.

P.S. Here's my copy of Schwartz-Bart.

Till Friday,

Linda

P.S.	When you write your letter after the first date:
	Do let your date know that you had a great time—and why.
	Do let your date know you'd like to see him or her again.
	Don't come on too strong. It was a "first" date, like in only "one."

After the Second Date

... suddenly I'm bright and breezy,
Because of all the beautiful and new,
Things I'm learning about you ...
—Oscar Hammerstein II, *The King and I*

ḣis ꜰeeLiṅgs

I t worked! I wrote to tell her how much I had enjoyed our first date and when I called, she agreed to a second.

We had a lovely dinner at Sign of the Dove. I specifically requested Table 2, which sits alone in a quiet alcove but provides a beautiful view of the flower-filled, skylighted center room. We were just far enough away from the pianist so that his melodies served as an undercurrent to our conversation without interrupting it. I wanted to get to know her better.

This time we shared more of our past. This time we discussed our individual hopes for the future. We discovered that we had much in common: interests, perspectives, likes and dislikes, and most important, values. We seemed to see life similarly—through the "same pair of eyes," I suggested.

I discovered she had a way with words and a super sense of humor. She was surprised to learn how relatively recent was my real success and how carefully I listened to what was said and what went unsaid. "You even hear the pauses," she complimented. There were differences, of course, but they were insignificant.

By the end of the evening, I had gotten to know her a lot better, and the better I knew her, the more I liked her. The next day, I sent flowers to her office. The card read simply:

I care,
Sid

I could have just waited awhile, then called for another date. But we were of a certain age and at a certain place in our lives which induced us to take relationships somewhat less than casually. Besides, I wanted her to know that I valued her highly and considered our evolving friendship important; and when you want someone to know something, tell them. Don't assume they can read your mind—or your heart. "I thought she knew how I felt," or "I thought she knew how much I cared," are the defenses of those who have already lost at love.

So I decided to write again. My letter wasn't designed to rush the relationship. Friendship must, I am convinced, precede real love. But I did want to make sure that I wasn't to be considered just another date, for I did not consider her "just another date."

Besides, once you establish yourself as someone who writes letters, your letters will be expected. That's just fine. It will prompt you to continue to communicate, and that is the single most important thing you can do if you want to build a successful relationship: continue to communicate.

his letter

Dear . . .

You are really unfair! If I have such a wonderful time with you, how will I ever be able to date anyone else? In fact, why would I want to?

I wish this evening had gone on forever. I think in my mind and in my heart it will. That's what "memorable" means. Was everything really that perfect or, when I am with you, does everything just seem that way?

It was a night of reaffirmation: you are as elegant, sophisticated, intelligent, and candid as I recalled. It was also a night of discovery: you have a wicked sense of humor, a terrific head for business, and the Big City hasn't spoiled you. There's plenty of "back home" and the artist you set out to be still there. And it's engaging and it's wonderful!

What I enjoyed most during the evening was our sharing stories of our childhood and our growing up, learning about each other's life, discussing our values and beliefs. In short, just getting to know each other better. That's really why I'm writing—to say I want to get to know you even better than that. You are becoming important to me.

There will be other dinners or shows, evenings at the homes of friends, a concert, a ball game—time to discover, time to explore. And all the while "getting to know you, getting to know all about you."

How lucky I feel that you have come into my life. . . .

Sid

ḣer feeliṇgs

Despite the changing ways of our society, women still tend to wait for men to make the first move, to ask for the first date. If after *he* asks, *she* accepts, and the date takes place, the woman often still is on tenterhooks, wondering: What did he think? Did he like me? Will I see him again? Will he call? She may still wonder even after he has asked for a second date and after a second wonderful time together. What she may not know is that he is probably wondering the same things.

How hard it must be to be a man. Males are expected to be strong, to be aggressive, to go after what they want. They are expected to do the asking, to be the initiators, to pursue, to make the plans, to buy the tickets, to bring the flowers, and to pay. Still. They are also expected to take rebuff or outright rejection without showing hurt and to be willing to risk rejection over and over again. Imagine being a man: What did she think? Did she like me? Will she see me again? Shall I call?

You can't be sure what he's feeling. But up till now, he's made all the moves. Why not give the guy a break and make the next move yourself? Why not ask him for the third date?

What if he turns you down? What if he says: "Sorry. I don't think the chemistry's right between us," or "I just don't feel I'm ready for a relationship right now"? Well, he might. Women often turn *men* down. *Women* say these things, perhaps believing that such phrases let someone down easy while precluding further involvement. Maybe the words achieve that effect, but they can still hurt. Being the one who does the asking is a risky and sometimes painful business.

Go on and ask. He may very well say yes. And you may again experience what a man feels in the same circumstances: happy you asked, delighted at the acceptance. In other words, human feelings, neither male nor female.

This time, take the entire responsibility. Make the plans, provide the transportation, and pay the bill. Your date doesn't have to be elaborate or costly. You're reciprocating, not making restitution. Think of something in which he indicated interest. Offer him options for time and day. And don't forget to tell him how much you enjoyed your second date.

ḣER LETTER

Dear . . .

Two on the aisle. Interested? I sure hope so. I can't think of anyone else I'd like to have share this show with me and I know how much you enjoyed their last performance. It's pretty short notice, but the tickets were a surprise from a friend and I couldn't be picky about the day.

After the show, I'd love to take you to V_____. They have a piano player who must have learned from Eubie himself. He's really tops. I never heard anyone get as much music from 88 keys. Sometimes I think he has four hands. You introduced me to chamber music. I'd like to offer you Willie the Lion, Memphis Slim, Commander Cody.

P.S.: Their menu is fantastic.

P.P.S.: Hope you will accept. If all this is fine, I'll be down to get you in a taxi Friday at 7:15. Your plans for us have been so delightful. Now it's my turn. Call me tonight or tomorrow and let me know.

Till then,
Linda

P.S. | When you write after the second date:

Do let your date know you continue to enjoy being with them—and why.

Do let your date know if you are beginning to consider this more than just casual; if you are beginning to take your date seriously.

Do let your date know you want to continue to get to know him or her—continue to see each other.

Don't start picking out colors for your wedding, and keep in mind that most deposits are nonrefundable.

I Must Have You

If I were tickled by the rub of love . . .
I would not fear the gallows nor the axe . . .
I would not fear the devil . . .
　　　—Dylan Thomas, "If I were tickled
　　　by the rub of love"

his feelings

G reat sex does not begin in bed. It begins in the head. It is the mind, not the elusive "G" spot, that brings on an orgasm. Successful lovers take the time to create an emotional base for a sexual relationship. They concentrate on their partner's feelings not on their anatomy.

Inexperienced lovers, typically the young, are almost invariably hurried lovers. The flame is quenched long before it has had time to generate real heat. Energy is a poor substitute for skill and patience.

Passion's fire ought to be kindled carefully and nurtured

slowly until it roars to life in a consuming conflagration of the senses. Of all the secrets of the adept lover—listening, responsiveness, spontaneity, creativity, enthusiasm—none is as important as resisting the temptation to rush, as enjoying the buildup. A skillful lover can make the anticipation as exciting as the realization. Prolonging that anticipation only heightens the thrill of fulfillment.

The earlier and extra courtesy and consideration, the unexpected compliment and unanticipated call to express your concern, the casual caress which is tender but not sexual, the myriad signals that convey how much you care for her are all precursors of superb sex later on.

As is the love letter that lets her know how very much you want her.

ḣis Letter

Dearest . . .

I cannot concentrate. Or, perhaps, I can concentrate but only on you. At work papers pass before me and I am nearly oblivious to their contents. My eyes wander from letters to reports only to come to rest on your photo framed in silver on the corner of my desk. How many times today have I brought it softly to my lips.

At meetings fervent debates rage about this item or that on someone's agenda, yet my notes consist of little more than your name—written over and over again.

The lack of sleep does not help. Restlessly tossing from side to side, I gave it up as helpless last night, slipped on a pair of jeans and sweatshirt, and went for a lonely walk. I am wound so tightly that I fear at any moment I may break.

If I close my eyes, I see your face before me. The sounds of silence are broken only by the remembrance of your laughter. Each breeze bears your aroma. No matter where I am, you are with me. *No, not merely with me, within me—so deep within me that I can no longer tell where I end and you begin.*

And I must, simply must be within you. I long to hold you close, to feel your heart beat in time with mine, to touch you and taste you, and have your excitement surround me. I ache to express this love which cannot be contained in one explosive, unforgettable moment. I want to hear the sounds you make as I bring you over the edge and into the realm of ecstasy. To please you as you please me, that is my dream.

I am yours and you are mine and we are one and must be one. I need what only you can give me - the fullness of your love. There is no other way.

Sid

P.S. | When you tell her you must have her:

Do put the focus on her. What it is about her that entrances you.

Do explain that your feelings are based on love not obsession.

Do, most important, convince her that your love will continue—that it won't end after you have "gotten what you want."

Do use as much romantic imagery as possible. You must convey a feeling of romance, not lust.

Don't set an ultimatum. "Either you do or I . . ." The only proper response to an ultimatum—and it is particularly apt in this case—is "Go fuck yourself."

After the First Time—When It Was Good

That's the wise thrush; he sings each song twice over,
Lest you think he never could recapture
The first fine careless rapture.
—Robert Browning, *Home Thoughts, From Abroad*

his feelings

There are at least three reasons why a love letter following the first sexual encounter between a couple might be a good idea.

First, such an experience marks a turning point of some considerable importance in a relationship. If the relationship is one you wish to see grow and develop, the drama and excitement of that occasion presents a meaningful opportunity to express your feelings and hopes for the two of you. It is fair to assume that your partner may have some second thoughts about "what happened" and wonder what effect it will have on the relationship.

This is your chance to let her know that lovemaking was the natural outgrowth of your feelings and will, inevitably, only draw you closer.

Second, even the most secure person will sometimes have doubts about their "performance" in bed and about how satisfactory their partner found the experience. If the experience was satisfying, why not put those doubts to rest and let your lover know she pleased you.

Finally, we are never more vulnerable than during lovemaking. It is the greatest gift of self that one human being can bestow on another. An expression of recognition and appreciation can go a very long way in parlaying one experience into a continuing, satisfactory relationship.

It's not an easy letter to write. Nothing worthwhile ever is.

ḣis Leᴛᴛer

Dearest . . .

I thought I knew the meaning of love. Last night you taught me a new definition. I never dreamed that anything could be as wondrous nor anyone as wonderful. You lifted me outside my body, I floated in mid-air and still have not returned to ground. Time stood still, the world and all its cares evaporated, the only reality was you. For one single solitary moment we danced with angels.

Few things in life meet our expectations, fewer exceed them. Whatever I hoped you would be like, you were more; whatever I hoped loving you would be like, it was more. And more. And more again.

One says "make love" and now I know why for we truly made love, created love, fashioned and refashioned it to fit our desperate need to express our feelings to their fullest. Love like that can never have existed before nor can I believe it ever will again until we are once more in each other's embrace.

Can I tell you what it meant to me, what it means to me? No, for I am neither a poet nor an artist. All I know is that we were two and now we are one, made one by the force of our love. May our oneness and our love flourish and may the glow within us warm our hearts forever.

For that glow, that very precious glow, is you.

Sid

her feelings

Lovers. "Loverly." And it is lovely because you've moved easily and naturally, mutually, to this stage, with your first act of lovemaking conducted in delight. And it is the ease and naturalness, the mutuality that makes the delight. No need to ask: "Was it good for you?" You both know it was.

Making love is our best expression of intimacy and caring. What a wonderful gift it is, one that we can continue to give again and again to our lovers. Each "gift" may not always be equal to the first time, but each expression of it is special, each expression can recall the first time.

Making love is also a commitment, an acknowledgment that you have become more than friends. But being friends first is what made your lovemaking natural. Continuing to be friends, as well as lovers, will keep it that way. The other side of the coin is that you must continue to be natural to be friends and lovers. Many women, and many men as well, don't talk much about sex. They may be operating under old inhibitions or prohibitions and be prone to easy embarrassment. They may regard lovemaking as something sacred, something one keeps to one's self, something reserved for night and darkness. Others may talk easily about sex—as long as it's not their own. They can joke in locker rooms. They can make light of it over drinks or coffee. They can discuss it with a doctor or therapist, but not with the most important person, their partner.

Why is it so hard to discuss sex? For most of us, it's fairly easy to engage in it. Easy to hug. Easy to kiss. Easy to experience the excitement. Easy to submerge yourself in it. But easy to talk about? No. Yet letting your partner know that you are happy with your lovemaking can reassure him, allow him to continue to be easy and natural with you, enhance his pleasure. Knowing what pleases each other can enhance your mutual delight. Openness in this case can be its own reward.

And let him know what pleases you about him as a total partner, not just a bed partner. What better time to begin to tell him than after the first time when it was good?

her Letter

Dear . . .

Did you eat the spaghetti this morning? Cold? Was it good? Save me some for tonight. But I want mine hot.

We certainly forgot about dinner fast. And after all that trouble. I think I ought to tell you that mineral oil won't do a thing for any cuisine. I think we should add a few items to your pantry. And to your refrigerator. Diet soda and Irish oatmeal aren't my idea of breakfast. Neither is spaghetti. By the way, just how long have you had that oatmeal?

Speaking of hot (I know we weren't speaking of it, but it's somewhere in this letter), whose son are you anyway? Vulcan's? We sure don't need to add anything to your repertoire. I think we may have disturbed some of your neighbors. I could hear windows opening up and down the air shaft. I wish I'd had a ski mask when

I left this morning. I swear even the doorman was smirking. I smiled back.

I don't think I'll get much work done today. I can't wait till tonight. Maybe we'll even finish the spaghetti.

So long, superman.

Love,
Linda

P.S. | When you write after the first time and it was good:

Do reassure your lover that your love continues stronger than ever.

Do let your lover know the hopes you have for the two of you and your future together.

Do express how much being together meant to you and how happy you were.

Do emphasize the romantic, the transcendental.

Don't emphasize the sexual. That's why they call it "making love."

After the First Time—When It Wasn't

All lovers swear more performance than they are able.
—Shakespeare, *Troilus and Cressida*

To every thing there is a season . . .
—Ecclesiastes 3:1

hIs fEELIngs

Lovemaking is a skill which must be mastered. It requires sensitivity, patience, and experience. Individual responsiveness varies as do needs and desires. It takes time for any two people to adjust to one another. If that is true outside the bedroom, it certainly is true inside.

But books, movies and television all raise our expectations unrealistically and make it seem as if each act of intimacy will be perfect from beginning to end. The problem is that when our expectations are not fulfilled, we rush to judgment, blaming either our partners or ourselves.

That's unfortunate, for there are few sexual problems that can't be resolved by better, more open communication—and practice. Yes, practice. It may not make "perfect" for perfect is but an ideal, but if a couple communicates what pleases them and if each of the partners is responsive to the other and puts into practice what they've been told, they will invariably be rewarded with a significantly improved sex life.

Never is this form of communication more important than after an initial sexual encounter which wasn't satisfactory. The entire future of the relationship may hang in the balance.

---

bis Letter

Dearest . . .

You know by now that I'm a romantic. I believe, truly believe, that "love conquers all." That even includes anxiety.

From the moment we first saw each other, we reached out. Tentatively at first, then more boldly. If in the beginning we moved slowly toward one another, in the last few weeks the pace quickened until we were positively racing. We were two people rushing to be one—one in every way.

Then, last night, there we were ready for fulfillment. If it wasn't in some respects what we had hoped, it was in others. We were both still new and strange at being alone together like that. I was in a hurry and you were anxious and both are understandable. But in a larger sense, we were both making a commitment of self to our relationship, both saying that we were willing to give everything we had to it and to each other.

To me that was the significance of last night and it is that which I will remember.

As time goes by and we grow more comfortable with expressing how we feel and what we need, as other opportunities arise to be alone so that we can continue learning about one another, we will both relax. Everything will become easier for both of us.

The important thing is not whether our first experience together was all either of us intended it to be. It is whether our love is strong enough to see us through. I think it is for I believe our love is a wonderful blend of consideration, understanding, tenderness and devotion. That's an unbeatable combination.

And in retrospect I want you to know that no matter what, I'd have rather held you in my arms last night than Venus, than Aphrodite, than any other woman in the world.

Until we are together again . . .

Sid

her feelings

All firsts are special simply because they're first, right? Well, what was so special about your first job interview? Your first traffic ticket? Your first flop with a recipe? Your first mistake?

They probably had two things in common: anxiety and nervousness. You weren't quite sure you had the qualifications for the job or you weren't prepared. You were in a hurry and you weren't expecting a cop. You'd never tried that recipe before- - or maybe you substituted an ingredient. You just didn't think. Results: No job. Trouble. No dinner. A mess.

The first time you and your partner make love *is* special. At least you hope it will be and want it to be. But sometimes sex too soon can make for an initial experience that isn't very special. You may care for each other very much. Maybe you've never made love before. Maybe you've had a lot of sex and found that it didn't lead to or at least wasn't a big factor in permanency in a relationship. You may be unsure about your ability to satisfy or gratify your partner until you've had more time together. In other words, you're not prepared and you're not sure you're qualified.

You don't know each other well, but he is pressing for greater intimacy. You are reluctant but afraid he'll seek a more willing partner. Or she is pressing, but you want this relationship to develop a little more; you're not sure what the direction of your involvement is. Or you both wanted to have a little more history together before getting sexually involved. These are tough new times. What's the hurry?

You're not very far into a relationship. Disagreements have already surfaced. *He* refuses to take part in many of *your* activities. *You* find *her* a little dull in company. You like jazz; he loves only '50s music. She hates all sports unless she's playing; you're an avid spectator. Maybe sex will smooth the edges and make the bad parts go away. Maybe it's the wrong recipe or the two of you aren't the right ingredients, and sex, no matter how great it is, won't ever replace food completely.

Scenario 1950s. First date: "I had a wonderful time." Second date: Kiss on the steps. Third date: Makeout/first base. (With minor variations.) Scenario 1970s. First encounter: "Let me grope your bod." No second encounter. (With variations.)

Scenarios 1990s. It's up to you. If you force intimacy on your relationship before you're ready, you may end up with a real mess. You can also back away, think about it, grab hold of your perspective, and agree to go back to your previous status for the time being.

]⊃ER LETTER

Dear . . .

There we were and then there we weren't. From now on, we'll know better. No second bottle of wine, Maybe not even the first.

We were in too big a hurry. No big deal. There's plenty of time ahead of us. I know this much: You know just where to touch me and just how. It was so wonderful and pleasurable, so warm and comfortable to be in your arms all night. Besides, we both got a good night's sleep.

We're friends. We felt relaxed and easy with each other from the get-go. What better prescription for love could two people have?

We jumped the gun a little, and the race is not always to the swift. I like to take things slowly anyway. It's a lot more fun.

I'll see you tonight. Bring orange juice.

Love,

Linda

P.S. | When you write to your lover after your first experience together wasn't satisfactory:

Do be reassuring, kind, gentle, and tender.

Do be reassuring, kind, gentle and tender.
(No, not a misprint. We know it appears twice.)

Do take the long-range view. People have to learn about each other's likes and dislikes. That's what time together is for.

Do explain that your love continues undiminished.

Don't overreact. Don't whimper. As T.S. Eliot reminded us, the world won't end with a bang.

Invitation to a Getaway Weekend

A book of verses underneath the bough,
a loaf of bread, a jug of wine,
and thou beside me, singing in the wilderness . . . ah,
wilderness would be paradise enow . . .
—Omar Khayyám, *The Rubáiyát*

his feelings

t's a wonderful idea! Escaping for a brief period of time together can bring a couple ever so much closer.

While dating is great fun, it is hardly the ideal way to learn about someone. So much of it is artificial. It tends to be limited in time, somewhat structured, and event or activity oriented. Really getting to know another person requires extended time together and the sort of letting your hair down that may not be possible in a date situation.

Also, if a couple is heading toward intimacy, I've always

thought it gentle and a bit elegant to plan a petit getaway for that significant first encounter. Spontaneously being swept into another's arms for lovemaking is unbeatable. But compared to merely "staying over for the night," the planned getaway can be a romantic delight. If you treat that first time as something special, chances are increased that it will be.

Even if a couple has been together for years, getting away every now and then can renew their romance. In familiar surroundings we are all likely to behave in set patterns. Change the locale, remove us from the pressures of daily life, and we are liberated—free to experience, free to explore each other anew. Tensions are reduced, strains forgotten, love revived.

For me the excitement of the getaway begins when I pick up the pen to write the invitation . . . .

ḣis Letter

Dearest . . .

I was over to Clarkstown Travel earlier today to pick up my airline tickets for that mid-May business trip I told you about. Travel agencies are "such stuff as dreams are made of." Waiting for Ellen to complete my booking, I began rummaging through the dozens of brochures on display. The Walter Mitty in me took over and I began fantasizing.

There we were on that beautiful beach in Anguilla toasting lightly . . . see us on that ski life in the Laurentians (How will I get down? I don't ski!) . . . What fun, we're climbing the pyramids outside Mexico City. There are certainly worlds enough but where does one find the time?

And yet . . .

I long to get away with you for awhile, even if it's just a long weekend. Someplace where we can be together. Someplace where we can be alone. A place where the telephone won't ring because no one knows we're there. A place we can go and leave the world and its cares behind. Our private Eden where I am Adam and you, my Eve.

I need seamless time with you: to see and to hear you more clearly than I can through the haze and the cacophony of everyday life. So much of you is still unchartered; there is so much more I want to explore, must explore.

On a quiet street in Lenox, perhaps the prettiest New England town I know, the Walker House accepts a few guests. It's the sort of place that lends you bicycles so you can pedal down country lanes, where tea is served on the veranda every afternoon. There are four-poster beds and fireplaces in every room and neighboring inns where we can dine by candlelight. Just down the way is a lake we can row across and all the fields invite us to picnic. I even have a kite we can fly if we've a mind to.

Let's . . . truly let's! Next weekend if possible, the weekend after at the latest.

I need you.

I need us.

Sid

ḣer ғeeliṇġs

You've been dating for several months, movies, beach parties and barbecues with friends, theater, dinners. You've spent a few nights together, but without much time for leisurely conversation, and you both have been either rushed to be off to work in the morning, to make an appointment, or to spend time with others. Until now, for the most part, he's the one who has paid for tickets and tolls, picked up the tab at restaurants. You'd like to reciprocate and you'd also like to have a little more time alone with him, perhaps allowing your relationship to progress a step forward. But a trip to Belize, even a week in Cape Cod is out of the question. Your time and your funds are limited. But your imagination is not. A getaway weekend, well planned, can occur in your own apartment or home.

When you make your plans, keep him uppermost. Think of things *he* enjoys. Keep the agenda loose, not too structured. You want the time to be comfortable and relaxed, not a charter flight with ten cities in three days. Leave breathing room for something he might want to add to your plans. Be flexible in your invitation. Offer him a choice of weekends. He may be very happy to accept, may have other plans or a heavy workload. Pick up his favorite foods and beverage, a selection of movies for the VCR. To ensure privacy, tell your friends and family you're off limits for the weekend except for emergencies. You're all set. Now for the invitation. Keep it light. No strong-arm tactics. You are not proposing marriage, just a fun weekend.

ḥER LETTER

Dear . . .

Congratulations! You, Mr. James Wonderful of Chicago, Illinois, have been selected as the winner in our Weekend Special Sweepstakes. The enclosed certificate entitles you to 72-hour occupancy in the VIP suite at 3716 Evergreen Parkway, Monterey Gardens, for any of the following weekends: June 15 through 17, June 22 through 24, or July 6 through 8.

Dress at our establishment is casual, and all activities are free. Guests are encouraged to participate in any and all events of their choice.

Snacks and meals are also free and all your favorites have been stocked. Kitchen and bar are open twenty-four hours a day.

If anything is missing or not to your satisfaction, we'll do our best to accommodate your wishes. A special selection of tapes and videos has been chosen for your listening and viewing pleasure. If there are any others you'd prefer, we will do our best to obtain them. Meantime, every effort has been made to ensure your comfort, satisfaction, and privacy.

We have no fixed check-in or check-out time. We hope, however, that you'll arrive as early as is convenient and stay as long as you can. We'd like to guarantee that nothing will disturb your casual, relaxed vacation, so we've turned on the answering machine and we'll screen all calls. If something comes up and you have to interrupt your time with us, we'll understand, but we hope it won't.

A few policies apply: No business is to be conducted on the premises for the period of your stay. No gratuities are accepted. Kissing, fondling, and otherwise gratifying and satisfying the hostess is strongly encouraged.

If none of the above times are convenient to your schedule, please let us know and we'll do our best to arrange a mutually satisfactory date for your weekend. We aim to please, and we'd love your company.

Love,
Linda

P.S. When you extend your invitation to a getaway weekend:

Do let it be known that the purpose is time alone together—time to get to know each other better.

Do recall the time pressures of everyday life and compare them to the quiet of a period away.

Do suggest places your beloved might enjoy.

Don't emphasize the sexual. It's not an assignation.

Don't extend the invitation unless you really want to—and can afford it. Resentment builds insidiously.

We're Going Too Slow

Had we but world enough and time . . .
This coyness . . . were no crime . . .
But at my back I always here
Time's winged chariot hurrying near.
—Andrew Marvell, "To His Coy Mistress"

his feelings

n my experience it is generally the woman who believes a relationship is going too slow, particularly if she is young, has never been married before, and spends an increasing amount of her time attending the bridal showers and weddings of her contemporaries. There is, after all, that imaginary clock ticking.

That's particularly unfortunate because the penalty to be paid for inappropriate compromise in choosing a life's partner is great. And although one can empathize when a young woman says she is "anxious to get on with" her life, good counsel advises that it's a long life with plenty of time to do it all. Today, women are starting their families ever increasingly later and with fewer frustrations of the "what I might have done" variety.

Nevertheless, it is a common complaint, "We're going too slow. He is afraid of *commitment*." (I hear that all the time!)

But there are men who feel the same way, too. He loves her and wants her for his wife, he is looking forward to being a Dad, he is afraid he'll lose her. (A poor reason, I think. Marriage is a contract and a moral commitment. It is not a chain. If love and a sense of commitment don't hold a marriage/relationship together, nothing will.)

In trying to explain why I may have believed a particular relationship was proceeding at the proverbial snail's pace, I've always been mindful of her need to be sure before forsaking options and making that all important commitment. I've also looked inward to make sure that what I was expressing wasn't a reflection of my own insecurity. I tried to let her know first, that I understand her hesitance; second, why I wanted us to proceed more quickly.

The letters have generally been well received and have served their purpose, i.e., prompted us to discuss our feelings thoroughly and try to reach an agreement about where we were going and when we hoped to get there.

Sometimes all it takes is that little extra assurance from the other person to alleviate our pacing concerns. Of course, at some point, it is perfectly legitimate to expect commitment or to move on . . . just not until you're satisfied you've given the relationship its due.

ḣis Leṫṫer

Dearest . . .

I've just returned from the gym, had a vigorous workout, and feel great. Left all my tensions in the locker room. Well, not all . . .

While I was on the treadmill, walking as fast as I could but not getting anywhere, I thought of us. We've been seeing each other for some time now and you know how very much you mean to me. You've told me how much you care, too. Yet, in many ways, we don't seem to be moving forward.

Forward to what? To commitment, to exclusivity, to building a life together. You are the only person I've ever known that I've wanted those things with. I can't imagine my life without you. And if you hadn't shown me that you feel about me as I do about you, perhaps I'd understand. But every time we talk about living together or marriage, you pull back.

I do understand that it's scary. For me, too. Truly, for me too. There's the fear that if we try for more than we have now, perhaps it won't work so maybe we should be content with what we have. There's the concern about a loss of freedom or independence. But without risk there is rarely a reward and without an investment there is never a return. Unless we risk what we have and invest ourselves in building our tomorrow together, the things that make life worthwhile will always be just beyond us.

We can't stand still while the rest of the world moves forward without slipping back. We've come so far together. If we hold hands tightly I know we can keep the pace.

The poet Andrew Marvell wrote:

> *Had we but world enough, and time*
> *This coyness, Lady, were no crime.*

He then goes on to explain:

> *But at my back I always hear*
> *Time's winged chariot hurrying near...*

I also hear that chariot. If you listen very carefully, I know you will hear it too. Time is not infinite for us. The days we waste apart will not come again and the chance for joy that each promises will pass us by.

Now is our hour.

> *Sid*

---

bER FEELINGS

Get on with it! What's the matter with him anyway? You've been together nine months and you feel like you're still holding hands, even if you long ago passed the handholding stage. If you're not already living together, you're almost never apart. You were willing to invest yourself completely because you believed this was a long-term commitment with a sure return. You discussed marriage, but with no specifics. Nevertheless, you found yourself leafing through *Bride* magazine. Both of you became more aware of couples with small children and agreed you wanted your own— some day. You talked about where you would live and the kind of home you always wanted.

For the last month, though, he has seemed preoccupied and withdrawn. He has suggested that it might be a good idea to spend some time with others or to have a day apart now and then. If you initiate any discussion about the future, he says now is not a good time to talk about it. Or else he changes the subject. When you ask him if anything is wrong, he denies it.

Is he backing out of your relationship? You don't know but you sure don't think he's all the way in. You begin to wonder if you're wasting your time. Where is the man you thought you knew, open, warm, and loving? Maybe he doesn't go the distance well. What does that bode for your future? Even your present?

Doubts about commitment are likely to surface just when your relationship is shifting stage to a greater commitment. Is he dragging his feet? That's not unusual, and you would be unusual if you didn't have some hesitation yourself about marriage, the state we all hope will be a lifetime state, despite the statistics.

Whether you're two months or two years into your relationship, the two of you probably have different timetables and they won't always mesh. The next step is negotiation. And it requires open channels of communication. You don't want to lose him and you don't want to issue an ultimatum. But you do want to clear the air and find out where you're stalled. First write down your own feelings and expectations. Only when you are sure of your own feelings will you be ready to write your letter.

hER LETTER

Dear . . .

Lately I feel we're not communicating very well. Perhaps you're aware of it too. It puzzles me because until now we've talked very freely.

Actually, we've made a lot of progress in a short time. We're very different, but our differences seem to open a new world for us rather than divide us. Whoever would have thought I'd learn to water ski or that you'd begin to enjoy nature walks? I hadn't been near a body of water bigger than a bathtub since I was six and you think that civilization ends where concrete stops.

We never run out of things to talk about, even if the debate gets pretty heated at times. We almost never agree, but we're worthy opponents for each other. Boredom certainly isn't our problem.

It's something else.

I think you started to get cold feet when we began to talk about marriage and a future together, but I'm not sure if that's true. It's hard to know what you're feeling unless you tell me.

It's certainly realistic to be concerned about taking the big step. Maybe it would help if you knew I have some reservations of my own. We ought to talk about it. We have to know where we stand. At least I must.

Love,
Linda

P.S. | When you write to say "we're going too slow":

Do keep in mind that you are telling your beloved how much he or she means to you—paying the highest compliment.

Do be empathetic. Let your partner know you understand and appreciate their concerns.

Do be totally reassuring. You are asking for a major commitment.

Do express the hopes you have for your future together.

Do let it be known that failure to move forward is in reality moving backward and that time is not infinite.

Don't give ultimatums.

Don't be afraid. If you are not prepared to accept "no," it is extraordinarily difficult to get a "yes."

CHAPTER 18

We're Going Too Fast

But joy is wisdom,
Time an endless song.
—William Butler Yeats,
    "Land of Heart's Desire"

Wait for that wisest of all counselors, Time.
—Pericles, in *Plutarch's Lives*

his feelings

As I noted in the previous chapter, I seem to hear frequently the lament, "He's a commitment-phobe." It may, in fact, be true of a particular person although there is probably a better way to express the complaint than relying on psychobabble. But, on the other hand, it is equally possible a fellow feels that a relationship hasn't progressed sufficiently to warrant making a commitment just now. Or, perhaps he feels he is being rushed unfairly and rebels. Of course, the very failure to commit after a reasonable period of time together is frequently a signal that this relation ship is not the right one. It is a signal that should not be ignored by either party.

It could also be that he loves her but, considering what is at stake, wishes to exercise a degree of maturity and wait until he is certain. I know that I have found myself in that position and, having been burned before, choose to put the lessons that I've learned into practice.

Whatever a man feels about commitment to a woman and to their relationship, it is only important that he express those feelings and let her know. Among other things, she has a <u>right</u> to know. The couple can then discuss that issue and those feelings and either resolve their pacing conflict or choose to go their separate ways. Once again, communication is the key.

More than once I have heard some woman say, "It's not so much that I want him to commit now as to know that he eventually plans to do so." An equally candid man, whose wisdom equals his candor, will realize that by putting his feelings on the table he can relieve a lot of the pressure both people feel.

It's probably easier to express those feelings in writing. They tend to be complex and writing gives one time to sort them out and try to make sense of them. One caveat: If after thinking about the relationship long and hard, a man decides he really does not intend to make this his permanent relationship, he really ought to let her know. It seems to me morally repugnant to simply string someone along for the mere convenience of it. We are, after all, talking about people's lives.

his Letter

Dearest . . .

These past few months have been a joy: the joy of discovery, of caring and sharing. I would not trade them for anything in my life. And if I cared for you less than I do, I'd let things go on just the way they have been without saying a word. It's because I do care so very much that I have to tell you what concerns me. Because I know you, I know you'll understand.

When my car is going too fast, I apply the brakes. If a horse I'm riding gallops and I don't feel comfortable doing so, I slowly pull in the reins. But what do I do with a relationship that has a momentum of its own when I believe that it is proceeding too quickly? The answer has to be, I tell you how I feel. To keep those feelings locked up inside me would be self-defeating. You'd only sense my withdrawal and be confused.

I don't want you to be confused. Instead, I want you to work with me to make what we have better. Our future has to rest on a more solid foundation than it does now if it is to last.

Sometimes, even though I think our relationship is wonderful, I wake up wondering how I got so deeply involved. I didn't intend to—not just yet. My work still requires the bulk of my time if I'm truly to make something of myself. To do that, I also have to continue my education. If our lifestyle is such that we spend almost all our time together or if I feel pressure to do so, I won't be able to give either my career or my education its due.

And when talk about living together or marriage comes up, when I know that we aren't ready for that yet no matter how exciting it may seem, I get the feeling that I'm losing control of my own life.

It's not that I want to see anyone else or be with anyone else. It's only that I want, I need, more time for me and for the things I need to do on my own.

There will come a time for us. You are the only person I want to spend my life with. It won't take forever for both of us to be ready to go forward together. But right now we've got to slow up a little, step back, give each other more breathing room, more thinking time. Burnout affects relationships too, and I don't want that to happen to us.

"Us" . . . that's still the nicest word I know.

Help me on this, will you? In the long run, it will only secure our future and mean greater happiness. Someone once defined "maturity" as "the ability to delay gratification." It may not be as much fun, but it is wise.

Sid

ber feeliηgs

He calls every day. In the morning before you leave for work, at work, at night. He has given you a gift on every possible occasion since you met, each with a card indicating his growing depth of feeling and attachment. It's been flattering and exciting. It's fun to be liked, loved, pursued. He's fun to be with and he's planned nice things for you to do together. He's pressing for more of your time and commitment.

You feel a little guilty. You haven't discouraged his calls or his attention. You like him and you don't want to give up the possibility of a relationship. Still, you aren't the one who initiates the calls or makes plans to be together. Sometimes, in fact, his calls are an intrusion. For whatever reason, you are new once more to the singles environment. You may have divorced. You are widowed. Or you have just ended a long-term involvement. You know you want to move more slowly, to test the waters, to be sure.

Pay attention to your feelings. Slow down. You don't have to move by anyone's timetable but your own. Examine the pattern of your involvement so far. What's his hurry? And what is your reluctance? Do you have any reason to suspect that his attentiveness is other than sheer liking for you and a desire to share his life with you? Do you give in to pressure easily instead of following your own inclinations or intuition? If the answer to either question is yes, put on the brakes. If the answer to both questions is no, you may be on the same track—except that you're riding the local and he's riding the express train. You can work it out by calling out the stops.

ḣer Lɛᴛᴛɛʀ

Dear . . .

The flowers are lovely. You never forget anything I say. Birds of paradise are fascinating. They remind me of quaint tropical creatures poking their heads out of jungle greenery. But I ran out of vases. The birds are everywhere, in my living room, bedroom, kitchen. Even the bathroom is bright with orange, blue, and green.

I really appreciate all your thoughtfulness, but I'm worried about your finances. A single white rose would have been just fine. I want us to slow down a little and enjoy the flowers in the garden (or the florist's) one by one.

I'm sorry I won't be able to go with you on Sunday. You plan such wonderful days that I hate to refuse. But I'm completely backlogged. I haven't paid my bills in a month, and the IRS won't be too happy with me if I don't file my return soon. I need at least a day or two a week to catch up on my "Musts" and "Ought Tos." My friends are beginning to think I've left the country. I'd like to have you meet some of them. I'll plan a dinner with two of them next week. I know you'll enjoy each other's company. Why don't you call me on Friday and tell me what evening would be best?

I'm sorry if I cut you off yesterday. I never have much time at work to have a relaxed conversation. There's always some emergency meeting or panic conference. I think it would be better if you catch me at home on my private line. Nobody at the office knows that number, and we can't be interrupted.

I am really looking forward to our trip to Nantucket, sailing, riding motor bikes. How lovely to be out of the city for a weekend. You chose another of my favorites. But then, you always do.

Until Friday,

Linda

P.S. | When you write to say "we're going too fast":

Do explain that you truly care for the one you are writing to.

Do explain how much that relationship has meant to you.

Do state that you want the relationship to strengthen and grow and that you both owe it to each other to give it time.

Do express your feeling that there is plenty of time and that you won't disappear.

Don't give ultimatums—not if you want the relationship to continue at *any* pace.

Where Are We Now?
Where Are We Going?

Love's not Time's fool
Love alters not with his brief hours and weeks . . .
—Shakespeare, Sonnet 116

his feelings

Ask! If you want to know something, and you have a right to know it, ask.

That would seem to be a fairly simple proposition. I am constantly surprised by the number of times some friend tells me they are uncertain where they stand in their relationship. It's a little like driving down a dark road without your headlights on.

Most of us invest a lot of ourselves in our relationships. We have an absolute right to know if the other person feels the way we do and wants the things we want. I'm not suggesting that discussing the state of a relationship is something a couple should do constantly. Nothing could be less productive, make you feel more self-conscious, or be more boring. Whenever I have had a romantic interest who was so insecure that almost every date ended with, "So where are we on this thing?", I've usually dreaded the ensuing conversation. But periodically it is perfectly understandable that one or the other parties wants, perhaps needs, some clarification.

Remember your teacher saying, "The only dumb question is the one you didn't ask." But ask the questions "Where are we now? Where are we going?" of the other person in your relationship—not of your friends. They don't know. Your partner does.

Or . . . your partner may not. Be prepared for that, too. Sometimes, "I don't know" is the most honest answer and I believe with all my heart that the most honest answer, framed in the least hurtful way, is always the best answer.

his Letter

Dearest . . .

I've been feeling somewhat insecure lately about our relationship and, because I trust you so, have decided to share those feelings with you.

You must know how deeply I care for you and how much I want us to build a future together. I've never known anyone as special as you nor been involved in a relationship as wonderful as ours. But, candidly, I'm not altogether certain you feel the same way about me or about us.

We both have a right to be fulfilled in all aspects of our lives - including our love life. If you don't see your future with me, then, as difficult as it will be for me, I'll step back so you can find that other special someone with whom to build your life. I, too, as sad as I will be at the loss of you, will eventually move on with my life.

It's not that I expect you to respond by saying that you are ready at this very moment to commit to me and to us. Rather, what I am seeking is some indication that you care for me as I care for you, that you would like us to continue to develop our relationship, and that you hope, as I do, that the future belongs to us.

I need to know that—almost as much as I need your love. But more than both I need to know just how you feel. Whatever the truth, and you've always told me only the truth, I'll deal with it.

One way or the other, you have been, and are, the highlight of my life.

Sid

ϸER FEELIⁿGS

Your relationship has become exclusive. You date only each other. When you plan something, you automatically include him. He does the same. Friends and family think of you as a couple, and address their invitations to both of you. If you show up alone anywhere, you're asked why you didn't bring him along. He keeps his bike, his camera, and his favorite bathrobe at your place, as well as enough clothes for a week. You don't have to pack when you "stay over" at his place. Everything's there but your cat. When you shop, you buy the foods he likes to have in the refrigerator. When you buy yourself a new toothbrush, you buy one for him as well.

You've taken vacations together. You've settled the little issues: what movies are best, how to spend your weekends. You've talked about the big issues: family, politics, religion—and the importance they have in your lives. You get along fine with your family. He's not as close with his. You're a Democrat and he's a Republican, but who cares? It's not a big election year. He goes to church every Sunday and you haven't been in one since

121

you were thirteen. None of these things has affected your relationship much so far.

Some things you have considered. He lives in the city and loves it. You feel a little claustrophobic after three days in his apartment. He works for a company with branches all over the world. Chances are he'll be in Hong Kong next September. You've just been promoted and it looks as though your career is finally moving in the direction you planned.

None of these things were of great moment before. He's certainly part of your present, a big part. But when you think of the "future," he's sometimes in the picture and sometimes not. After all, you're not engaged. You haven't really discussed commitment.

Just the other night at dinner, he asked casually, "Have you ever thought of having children?" Surprised, you answered, "Once in a while," and changed the subject quickly. Now he looked surprised. You both were uncomfortable, and spent the rest of the meal in light chatter. As you drove home, he said he couldn't stay the night. Then he added, "I've got some papers to work on before I meet my boss in the morning. Looks like I'll be going to Hong Kong sooner than I thought. Maybe you'd like to see the Far East. Think about it." And do you ever. You hadn't realized how much of his future included you. You're happy and excited. Maybe stunned is more like it. Until now, you've been riding the wave of a nice steady relationship, with a lot of potential but an open door in front of you. You've never been farther from home than Montreal. Your own plans are just taking shape. Are you ready to leave your job and your home? Are you ready for marriage and a lifetime commitment?

Whoa! You don't have to decide your whole life tonight or even next week. He's a little ahead of you, that's all. This is a big turning point. Take all the time you need to decide. If your decision is to let him go alone, you may be risking your relationship and any future for the two of you. And maybe not. If he loves you, he'll understand and will wait. But you do have to let him know your decision. Remember, planes fly to Hong Kong every day. And you can always write him a letter.

her Letter

Dear . . .

This has been a very difficult decision to make. I haven't slept tonight. I picture my rooms without you in them. I imagine myself opening your door, calling your name, and hearing no answer. It's so hard to contemplate. I'm so used to seeing you almost every day, to our phone conversations at night. We've never been separated for more than a few days.

How I will miss you. But I just can't come with you at this time. My promotion means a lot to me. I have worked so long for it. It means not only a lot more money, but autonomy and a chance to travel as well. If I were to leave now, I think I might regret it in the future and resent you for it.

I'm very happy for you. M_____ evidently thinks very highly of you, but I have to confess I wish it hadn't happened quite so soon.

I couldn't take it all in last night. It was too fast. By three o'clock this morning I felt a little better. My vacation is due in a month, and I have a sudden strange longing for the mysterious East. And your company will have to schedule you back here at least once every six weeks. At least they did when you were based in Holland. Honey, you're not going to get a chance to miss me. Maybe you'll even be sorry you gave me your new address. And by next fall, maybe it will be mine, too—that is, if you'll still have me. Meantime, who's going to drink all that diet soda?

Love,

Linda

P.S. | When you write to discuss the state and direction of your relationship:

Do begin by telling your beloved why you feel uncertain.

Do note how much the relationship means to you.

Do express your hopes for your future together.

Do state specifically what it is you need from the other person —a reaffirmation of their love, an indication that they share your hopes for the future, a commitment now. If you don't frame the question clearly, you can't possibly get the answer you're seeking. (Although it may not be the answer you want.)

Don't be timid. This is an issue that affects your life and future. If you are not for yourself, who will be for you? And, if not now, when?

I'm Falling in Love with You

For, you see, each day I love you more,
Today more than yesterday and less than tomorrow.
—Rosemonde Gérard, "L'Éternelle Chanson"

his feelings

T his is the most important chapter in the book, yet it concerns the second most important love letter you can write: the one in which you tell someone that you are falling in love with them. The only love letter that is more important is the one that follows: "I love you." But why adopt a two-stage approach? Why not hurry past "Go," collect the reward, and proceed immediately to "I love you"?

The answer involves the single most significant issue in building a successful relationship: parallelism. For a relationship to succeed, both parties must want it to succeed and in about equal measure. They must both care about their relationship and each other to the same degree. If one person gets too far ahead of the other, that is, if one cares significantly more than the other, an imbalance occurs which not only destabilizes the relationship but endangers its very existence.

That isn't to say that both people must always be "in the same place" in the relationship. Rather, if you feel yourself getting in "too deep," caring a lot more than your partner, you either have to pull back or seriously question whether you should (*not* can) continue with it. This morning a friend told me of a relationship she was in for years, one in which the fellow never was able to make a sufficient commitment toward marriage. (I've heard the same story a number of times where the issue wasn't even marriage, merely some form of permanence or exclusivity. And it hasn't always been the man who was the hesitant one, either.) Such a relationship has almost always gone on too long. One party cares in a way that the other does not understand, or loves with a love of which the other is simply incapable.

Parallelism at least requires that you be moving in the same direction. You don't always have to be in the same place at the same time, but you should be moving toward a common goal. If one party gets too far ahead or if one or both stop their forward momentum, it's probably time to change direction. That's painful and difficult, I know. I've been there. But it is necessary and ultimately less painful than staying in a relationship that is not developing as you want it to.

Yes. People do change—but they have to do it on their own. As the woman I've loved most in my entire life once said, "There are but two truths: you can't change anyone and people change." Of course, it may be that "your" person won't change. Nor is time a complete irrelevancy.

What has all this got to do with writing a letter to tell someone: "I'm falling in love with you"? Just this: It's the second biggest statement, the second-biggest exposure of your most vulnerable self you can make. Before you write such a letter, make sure of two things: first, that you absolutely mean what you are about to write; and second, that you are not running too far ahead of your beloved. You have both a responsibility to yourself and to your other. You want to be as sure as you can that your letter will be welcome, not upsetting. You want the reaction to your letter to be, "It's wonderful. This is what I've been waiting for." You *don't* want it to be: "Oh, oh. Look what I've gotten myself into. I don't want to hurt him (her)."

But that's the value of the two-stage approach. It clearly signals how you feel, where you "are coming from," where you're "at," and, most important, where you are heading. It does not, however, say you are there yet. Thus, it gives the other person two important things to which he or she is entitled: an honest statement of your developing feelings and an opportunity either to respond in kind (mutual commitment) or to indicate that although your feelings are appreciated you are moving too far ahead just now (lack of parallelism), or, perhaps, to let you know that he or she doesn't or likely won't feel the way you do. Even if that's the case, at least you'll know it at a stage when you should be able to extricate yourself from the relationship without major hurt.

If you jump right to "I love you," in a way you are setting up an ultimatum—requiring a yes/no response. By letting the other person know your feelings as they develop (continuous communication), you give him or her a chance at least to adjust the intensity of the relationship, restore parallelism, and keep things moving forward together.

The letter that follows is one I will not mail. Instead, I'm going to give it to her when we go out for my birthday. I want her to know how I'm beginning to feel, but I also want to know whether she feels as I do—that she's where "I'm at."

his LETTER

Dearest . . .

There was a time in my life when I believed that whoever in a relationship cared the least was the strongest. I came to realize that whoever dared to care the most was the bravest. It is, after all, risky to put your emotions on the line. It is especially risky to be the first to express your deepest feelings. I think it's a risk worth taking.

Ever since we met, the world has seemed a different, a better place. I keep checking the Science Times and am surprised that there's been no report of the sky being bluer, the stars brighter this year. Am I the only one to have noticed?

Children surely play more nicely now, there are a lot more robins this season, and courtesy seems more prevalent as I roam about town. I'm certain of it.

I even recall that once upon a time I might have had a bad day, lost faith in myself, or doubted the future. But not since the day I met you.

Will I have to get a pilot's license now that I float down the street without my feet touching the ground? Will I be committed? That's what happens, I'm told, to people who smile all the time.

Get the idea? You've changed my life, you've changed my whole world. I looked for you so hard, so long, that now that I have finally found you it's like a miracle. You are my miracle. You are beautiful and you are bright, sensitive and intuitive, gentle and generous—and you are the kindest person I have ever known,

If God had come to me the day before we met and asked me to define the person I was searching for, I would have described just exactly who you are. Is it any wonder then that I find myself falling in love with you?

It's a steep and slippery slope I'm on. If I let myself fall, I'll *fall hard and I'll fall fast. I'm not afraid, but I'd like to know you'll be there to catch me. If not—or if not just now—let me know and I'll break the fall. I can do so now but perhaps not in a little while.*

It is a little dangerous to open yourself up so completely—to tell another how much you care. And I may not be as brave as I should like to think. But, oh, if you do feel as I do, what joy we are destined to share together. "Together"—isn't that a beautiful word?

Sid

ᚻER FEELIᚾGS

Falling in love is a universal phenomenon. It is the wild elation that strikes us like a bolt from the blue according to the French— a *coup de foudre*, a thunderclap. Italians say they they see their loved one's image "in their soup"; it follows them everywhere night and day. An Israeli might say, *"Ani mitgagat lekha"* ("I'm crazy for her"). A Spaniard says exactly the same thing: *"Estoy loco por ella."* A Jamaican phrases it in slang as "Me a dead fi' it." The Chinese describe the staggering feeling as

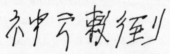

or blind love ("You make me dizzy: my head is spinning").

In America, we have dozens of expressions for the feeling: head over heels, bewitched, besotted, enchanted, captivated, in a dream, mad about, crazy about, wild about, insane for, infatuated, smitten, swept away or off our feet, out of our heads.

All these expressions imply a magic crazy state over which we have no control, one that is beyond the reach of reason. And that's exactly what it is: unreasonable. Still, it feels so good that we don't care. When we are bewitched, bothered, and bewildered, we don't want psychologists to explain it away as a mere chemical attraction and reaction. We'll take the excitement and the thrill, thanks.

No doubt about it. The feeling's so great that we find ourselves wondering where it went when it passes. It always does because it isn't real. If we're not wise, we keep trying to recapture the thrill in an endless series of relationships that never go beyond the initial stages. If we're smart, we work at the present relationship, getting to know our partner at deeper and even more satisfying levels. Now we're standing on our feet, with our wits about us. No more dream lover, but a walking, breathing human, with foibles and lacks and dreams, much like us. Yet the attraction is stronger, and more realistic. We're beginning to stand in love.

ḣer Leᴛᴛer

Dear . . .

It doesn't make sense. I might as well be sixteen. It might as well be Spring. I long to hear your voice, to feel you touch me. You're in my every moment, just as though you were standing next to me. When I wake, as I prepare for my day, through the day until I see you, I find myself saying your name as though just saying it were a spell to bring you to me. When you are due to arrive, I catch myself lifting the curtain to catch a glimpse of you.

That really makes me feel sixteen again. I can hear my mother's voice: "Sister Anne, Sister Anne, is he coming?" Later, she told me that the words came from the grim tale of Bluebeard, who killed a raft of women before Anne and her sisters, his prisoners, finished him off and ended his reign of terror.

Don't panic. You don't have to arm yourself to come to my "castle." Nothing but welcome awaits you. My mother was giving me a different warning: not to be so anxious for someone's arrival, not to submerge myself in another person so greatly that

I lost my perspective.

But I don't think I have lost it. I can reel at your touch and drink in the sight of you like any lovestruck child. I can dream of the voluptuous curve of your mouth and the hard flow of your body, and your etc. I can see you everywhere, in my imagination, in my coffee, in my today and tomorrow. At the same time, I know that I didn't dream you up. The love I feel for you is not imaginary and not that of a sixteen-year-old. I know this because I know you.

I know that when you give your word, I can count on it. I know that when I need your help, you are quick to offer it and you stay till the job is done. I know that you approach everything in life with devotion and attentiveness.

I know these things from watching you, being with you in myriad daily circumstances. You keep an even keel, never getting upset at minor annoyances. You are flexible and open to new events. You mix easily and naturally with my friends and family. You are courteous and kind.

I know I can trust you with my feelings, anything that spins into my head. I never have to censor my thoughts or words, or wonder if you'll misunderstand what I say. Who else could I tell of Bluebeard and love in the same letter?

Because of this trust in you, I know I can trust my own feelings. No question—I was wild about you three seconds after you said hello for the first time. But my head's on straight and my vision is clear. I didn't just fall in love: it was free fall. Now the parachute has opened and I want to keep on floating forever.

Love,
Linda

P.S.

When you let someone know you are falling in love with them:

Do make certain you mean what you are about to write. It is one of the most important statements you can make. You are dealing with another person's heart and are likely to be believed.

Do think carefully about whether the other person is at the same stage in the relationship as you are. A premature declaration of love can thwart a promising relationship.

Do let your beloved know what it is about them that made you fall in love.

Do let your beloved know how they make you feel— why you are sure it is love.

Do express your hopes for the future.

Don't gush. Don't lock your reader into a "yes" or "no" response. Leave them time to reflect and consider.

I Love You

Drink to me only with thine eyes,
And I will pledge with mine;
Or leave a kiss but in the cup
And I'll not ask for wine.
                    —Ben Jonson, "To Celia"

his feelings

They are the most important words that can be said or written: I love you. Those words raise expectations, fulfill dreams, and create futures. We all long to love and to be loved, and most of what we do in our lives is aimed at satisfying that longing. Without love, there is no life worth living.

Love alone may be insufficient to assure the success of a relationship, but it is the indispensable element. Without that spark, there can be no fire; without the fire, there can be no glow.

For my last birthday, Ilana gave me a book to write my thoughts in. The first entry is but two sentences: "I believe in love.

I believe in other things as well but even if I didn't it would be enough." I stand by that—and by this: I believe that if you placed all the good in the world on one side of a scale and love alone on the other, the balance would tip toward love.

There is no one definition of love that is right for everybody. For each of us the word has a somewhat different meaning. What one person means by the words "I love you" may not be exactly what another person understands them to mean. Do they mean I want us to see each other only? I want to marry you? I'll leave my spouse for you? You can do no wrong that I won't forgive? Of all the expressions one might expect to be unambiguous, "I love you" should rank way up there. Not so. Therefore, when you write "I love you," it's a very good idea to let your beloved know what the words mean to you and what you hope they will mean for both of you. Or, to put it another way, simply including the words "I love you" doesn't make it a love letter.

I have given a lot of thought to what I mean when I say "I love you," For me, love is the ultimate commitment to another's happiness. It makes the welfare of that person the supreme value of your life. It is the expression of maximum devotion and highest regard. It is the essence of getting by giving. Its hallmarks are caring, tenderness, trust, honesty, fidelity, and respect. It is selfless, boundless, free-flowing, and unconditional. And, at its best, it is mutual.

How saddening it is that so many use the word "love" indiscriminately or hesitate to use it at all. For some, the word seems to be a currency that is used to pay for sex or things or favors. Others simply bandy the word about as if it had no special significance at all. I've surely been guilty of both. For years, I felt that under many circumstances the word was expected of me. Only slowly did I come to realize that the more honest expression, "I care," was enough to say—and then only if I meant it.

There are two problems with using the word "love" loosely.

First, as with so many other things, if it is used too commonly it loses its value so that when you really want to use it the word has become meaningless. Second, its careless use hurts those who believed you meant what you said.

Only slightly less troubling are those who fear commitment and thus avoid using the "L" word altogether. Perhaps love spells obligation and obligation means responsibility. They want to be "free," we are told. What they wind up free from, however, is love itself, because without commitment, there can be no real love.

When you are truly in love and willing to commit your life to another, it's like reaching a goal, concluding a search—the lifelong search for love that we all engage in. The temptation is to shout out "Eureka!" When that love is reciprocated, the expression of your love can be joyful. It is also a solemn occasion. Joyful and solemn—rather like a wedding: the "marriage of true minds" that Shakespeare proclaimed.

Saying "I love you" benefits from spontaneity and may be rewarded by an immediate response. But taking the time to put your thoughts and feelings in a love letter provides you with an opportunity to express yourself more fully, effectively, beautifully, and memorably. And if any letter you ever write is likely to be saved, this one is.

Recently, I was asked the number of women to whom I've said "I love you." "Rather more than I should have," I confessed, though the confession does not absolve me from the wrong. But there have been those times when the love I felt was so genuine, so overwhelming, that I simply had to express it. I've generally chosen to do it with a letter.

The letter that follows is a re-creation of one I wrote from Tel-Aviv to a girl in Jerusalem. I was returning home. She was staying to study. I cannot tell you how our story turned out because we are still living it.

ḣıs Lεττεʀ

Dearest . . .

I am sitting on my terrace overlooking the Mediterranean. It is late afternoon and the sun is just beginning to descend. In a few hours, I will chase it westward and home. Home? Home is supposed to be where the heart is , and I am leaving my heart here with you. For years I have said that part of my heart was always in Israel. Now all of it is.

Can it really be only a month since we met? I remember that first day so clearly. Shulamith was conducting the first assembly. "You're a lawyer from America? So meet a lawyer from Canada— maybe you'll start a partnership!" And there you were radiating the most magnificent smile with which anyone was ever blessed. How often in the weeks that followed did I look forward to seeing that smile. It brightened my days, it warmed my nights.

It seemed that it would take forever before we had an op- portunity to be alone, to talk, to get to know one another. Either we were always surrounded by others, or the moment we saw each other, others would suddenly appear. But there were moments, and we made the best of them: a study session here, a walk there, a quiet meal. Slowly, tentatively, we reached out; almost shyly, surely with hesitation.

You were not easy to get to know. There is a rhythm, a melody to each person's life. Some are simple tunes, pleasant enough though not particularly memorable. Others are marked by dis- sonance and are best avoided. But you, you are a symphony rich with major themes, given color by interwoven minor ones. Complex yet harmonious—appealing to the mind and to the heart. Never had I met someone so worth getting to know.

But get to know you I did. I discovered enormous strengths and touching vulnerabilities, a confident you and a self-doubting one, a kinetic person and one who could sit under a tree and study the petals of a flower endlessly, a scholar and an artist.

And I learned to love them all, for they were all you, and I'd never known anyone like you. I've known women I've respected before and, yes, I've been in love before. But never had I felt so much of both—respect and love—at the same time and for the same person. So I made my big mistake: I declared my feelings too soon. But my error was one of judgment, not dishonesty, for my feelings were as true as love ever was true.

You withdrew and I was in anguish. Until that last day as I was signing out and you came up behind me, tapped me gently on the shoulder and, as I turned, said simply, "Hold me." Never, not even if some day God points to Heaven's portals and says, "You may enter," will any words mean as much to me as your "Hold me."

For I so love you that I should rather hold you from now until the end of time than do anything else. For you alone was I given arms; for you and only you do I have these lips. My tongue is there but to please you with its praise, my eyes to dwell upon your beauty only. I truly believe that I was created for you—and you for me.

I recall having read that in Heaven before we are born we are each possessed of a whole soul. But the process of being born on Earth is so difficult that each of us can only make the journey with but half a soul. Thus, we are destined to spend our life searching for our other half.

My search seems to have gone on forever. Surely there were times I thought the "fit" was right or that I could make it right. But not until I met you was I sure it was right because not until you did I ever truly feel whole. You are the one who has made me whole again.

I'm a man and men are "supposed" to be brave but with you I could express my fears. I'm a man and men are "supposed" to be strong, but with you I could confess my weaknesses. And all my life I have been praised for succeeding at what I did well, but I felt free to tell you the things I'd still like to try even though I might not succeed at them. In short, with you I could be completely myself, without pretense and without artifice, and miracle of miracles for you that was enough!

I say I love you, and I mean I love you, but I mean more as well. I mean I want to be there for you always and want to know that you will be there for me. Without limitation, without exception. I mean that I want us to share each other's life, each other's destiny. As for me, your happiness, your well-being will become essential parts of my own happiness, my own well-being. I mean that I look forward to the time we marry, have a family, and experience the joy of being one.

You do not have to do anything to earn my love. I give it to you freely. You do not have to do anything to keep it. It is yours forever. It will never lessen, it will surely never disappear, but if you nurture it, its growth will be boundless.

I'm so grateful to have found you!

It's about time to leave for the airport. How I will survive the next few months until you return, I do not know. But we'll write. . .and phone. . .and plan. . .and dream. The sweet dreams of lovers.

Shulamith said, "Maybe you'll start a partnership." Little did she know. . . .

Until you are in my arms once more, I'll hold you in my heart.
Shalom

---

her feelings

Three little words. What do they mean? Is it "your eyes of blue, your kisses, too"? The "Sweet Mystery of Life"? Webster's says: ". . . a deep and tender feeling of affection or an attachment or devotion to a person . . . a strong liking for or interest in the object of such liking . . . a strong, usually passionate, affection based in part on sexual attraction . . . the person who is the object of such affection." Other dictionary definitions vary only slightly, but libraries, even warehouses could be filled with the seemingly endless tomes that define and purportedly explain love in all its facets. The syllables would stretch in an infinite line, to Alpha Centauri and back, to the limits of a limitless universe. One thing's sure, your definition is not mine and mine is not yours—a reasonable facsimile maybe, but not the same. Thank goodness, or we'd all be pursuing the same object, not the same objective.

The definition of love remains a sweet mystery. It's not just a strong affection, passionate and sexual. If it were, we'd never get past our first object of sexual desire. And let's consider the word "object." Bad choice. Your loved one is the object of, the recipient of, your affections, but is not an object, not a possession, a thing. If we keep the "deep and tender feeling," and the "devotion" and add "abiding," we are getting closer to an approximation of love. What makes us continue in love—not falling in but standing in love—are the abiding characteristics of the person we love. Physical qualities fade. So do energies. You fell in love with his mane of hair and his gorgeous body. But his concern and devotion to your interest are what remain when his hair thins. His concern, tenderness, and strength of character endure even if he can no longer carry you in his arms. Now he carries you in his heart and mind. You have a growing sense of familiarity, of family, of unity and mutuality. A comforting and peaceful awareness of security.

These feelings are what Shakespeare termed "a marriage of true minds." Nonetheless, love is not "an ever-fixed mark." Love can be deeply shaken. Love alters. Love has stops and starts, crises and stalemates. Sometimes the feeling of unity dissipates. Initial goals and roles change. So do circumstances. Partners change. And change in a partner can be threatening or frightening, demanding that we reassess ourselves, our positions and expectations. But a healthy dash of tolerance and respect for each other will help you past these hurdles.

The first heady rush of love persists to differing degrees for different partners. Some keep the elation forever. How lucky they are. And how lucky and how smart you are if you recognize and affirm the abiding qualities in your lover that make you persist in your love for him.

ḥer Letter

Dear . . .

I love you. Let me count the ways.

<u>One</u>: I like you. You are my friend, someone I can talk to, tell my secrets to, show my entire being to, in confidence—my willing and sympathetic listener, my safe and trusted haven.

<u>Two</u>: You are adventure itself. You have so much curiosity about so many things that your mind is never still. You are open to the moment—a boatyard, a beach, a strawberry patch, and you want to stop and explore. I'm never sure what our day will hold, what plans will go by the board, what new people I'll meet, or what new project or goal you will share with me. I do know I won't be bored.

<u>Three</u>: You see things with clarity and precision, and you teach in the same way, logically and sequentially. And always creatively. You lead your law students to understanding an offer of a unilateral contract by reciting a song lyric: "A million baby kisses I'll deliver, if you will only sing the Swanee River." Who could forget that? No wonder they like you and crowd your classes. No wonder I enjoy your explanations of things unfamiliar to me.

<u>Four</u>: You keep the child in you alive, curious and wondering. Children respond to you without inhibition. Here is a "grown-up" who takes them seriously, who answers their questions with gravity, who draws them out and is never condescending. They

look forward to your visits and hate to see you leave. What a wonderful father you will be.

<u>Five</u>: You take me seriously. You're not as patient with me as you are with students or children. You expect more of me. You always want the best I can give. But your expectations are an incentive; you are clearly interested in seeing me progress in my work and my activities. And you offer me active support in that progress.

These are not the only reasons I love you. I could list your spontaneity, your quickness to forgive, to dispel anger, your persistence in finishing difficult tasks, your wit, your vivid imagination, your contempt for pettiness.

Does this sound like a resume? Let me add that you are my lover, passionate, exciting, and inventive. The one who fills my thoughts, my nights and days. Not my first love, but by far the best. I want you to be my last, my only love.

Yours,
Linda

P.S. | When you write to say "I Love You":

Do make certain you mean what you say. It is *the* most important statement you can make to someone.

Do think carefully about whether your timing is right.

Do let your beloved know why you love them or what it is about them that you love.

Do let your beloved know how they make you feel and why you are so sure it is love.

Do let your beloved know your hopes and plans for your future together.

141

Do give your words wings. Be as expansive as your love.

Don't hesitate because of a *fear* of rejection. Nothing ventured, nothing gained.

Why You Are So Important in My Life

It is only with the heart that one can see rightly;
What is essential is invisible to the eye.
—Antoine de Saint-Exupéry, *The Little Prince*

ḣeR ꝼeeLiꝛGs

O nce you've told someone you love them, you may think you've said it all. After all, aren't those the words we all long to hear? But just repeating the words "I love you" at intervals isn't enough. It states your feelings, but it doesn't tell your loved one what you value in him or why he is important to you. When you first met, it may have been his great dancing or his square shoulders that excited you. Now you have been together for some time. You've shared myriad and mundane moments. You've had Thanksgiving dinner together with *your* family, Christmas dinner with *his*. You've been stuck in a traffic jam together.

You've seen him when he first wakens in the morning. He's nursed you through the flu. It's not the first flush of romance any more. It's better than that. You've progressed from the Outer Core to the Inner Core. This is a real human lover to whom you're responding on a deeper level. And it's not his dancing or his square shoulders that excites you. It's his friendliness and ease in company. His calmness in a tight situation. His cheerfulness at 7:00 A.M. His tenderness. And it's time to tell him about it with more than a kiss or three little words.

her Letter

Dear . . .

I can't imagine my life any more without you. Who else would sing Gershwin while showering? Even if he did, would he also know "A Wandering Minstrel"? And be able to carry a tune? And would he take a piano break instead of a coffee break? Would he know the importance of won-ton soup after a bad day and that it had to be Cantonese, not Szechuan? Would he know I need a seat belt when I sleep at night? Would he grab my hand and zip me off to the boatyard to fantasize about the day we'll pack it in and take off for Tahiti? Would he pick strawberries with me in July or pop popcorn at two in the morning?

I doubt it. He might even think I was a nut. Or else he'd take 32 vitamins before each meal and listen to nothing but 60s oldies.

I could live without Gershwin and even without won-ton. What I could never do without any more is the gentle encouragement you give me when I have a problem that seems insurmountable, the way you not only listen to me but the way you take it in, the way you hear me. You listen to children in the same way. When you play the "Different/Same" game with Ryan and Drew, they are almost breathless in their desire to give the best answers and then

144

to ask a good question in turn. If you don't come along on the visit, they're truly disappointed: "Next time, bring _____! We'll fly our kites again."

I love our long drives together. You're such a calm driver, no matter what the road or traffic is like. But what's even better is your willingness to try a new road and to stop at unexpected places—a beach, a garden center.

More than anything, I can't imagine not having you to talk with, to share not only the events of the day and the world, but also to figure out the motives of characters in movies, old and new; to discuss the best word to express a thought; to delight in the way children phrase things; to add to our private language just those phrases.

You enlarge my world and my life. You not only taught me about biking in New York, sailing on the Sound, chick-pea salad, and California rolls; you also brought me gentleness, tenderness, and an exciting head tour. What's more you keep the child in you alive and you let me do the same. Here's to wonder and curiosity, and long life and love to us.

With all my love,
Linda

P.S. | When you write to tell someone why they are important in your life:

Do particularize. It's not just any person who has certain characteristics, it's this unique person who has become important. Remember the song "My One and Only."

Do express your gratitude, your joy in the relationship.

Do state how your beloved adds to the *quality* of your life.

Don't appear dependent. It's not an "I need you because I can't" letter. It's an "I can and you are important to me anyway" letter.

After the First Disagreement

Mutual forgiveness of each vice,
Such are the gates of Paradise.
        —William Blake, "Gates of Paradise"

Love consists in this, that two solitudes
protect and touch and greet each other.
        —Rainer Maria Rilke, *Letters to a Young Poet*

bis feelings

♦t might have been over whose parents to spend the holiday with
or whether to continue seeing that other couple as frequently.
Perhaps the issue involved where to spend your vacation,
whether you really needed to purchase such an expensive that
when you had both "agreed" to get a less expensive this, or one of
a dozen other fairly minor matters. Whatever the question, you've
had your first real disagreement.

Did you really think you'd both go through life in perfect
accord, seeing everything exactly the same and always agreeing?

Pollyanna! You're not in a relationship with a mirror, with yourself That's a totally separate individual standing by the window, staring out, wondering why you are so stubborn.

Let it pass. There are big issues in life and odds are this wasn't one of them. Don't make the mistake of looking at everything through a magnifying glass. A tremor does not an earthquake make.

My father, Meyer Bernstein, used to say that if you woke up in the middle of a desert with no one around for hundreds of miles, sure as can be someone would appear by noon to cause you trouble. "Don't cause yourself trouble."

It was no big deal. Refuse to let one passing cloud spoil the sunshine of an otherwise rewarding relationship. Come on, now, drop her a line and put the whole thing into perspective.

ḣis Lecceʀ

Dearest . . .

Gee, what I really wanted in a relationship was someone who always agreed with me even when I was wrong; someone who always said "yes" even when the answer should have been "no"; someone who pronounced "tomato" and "pyjamas" the right way—which is to say, my way.

Nonsense!

What I wanted, and what I found, was a separate, sovereign, intelligent and perceptive human being with her own thoughts, her own insights, and her own opinions. I wish I were really as certain or secure about everything as I sometimes seem. Knowing that you're there to discuss things with, to work things out with me, to learn from, really helps.

I'm proud that you are in my life—this bright, beautiful independent person. It's only natural that on occasion we will

disagree about something. There is, however, one thing about which we will never disagree: how much we love each other.
                                                   Sid

her feelings

Watercolor artists often "mask out" areas of white paper until they have filled in the back-ground of their painting. They then lift off the film and add the finishing touches.

If only we could do that with people!

We try. We all have a preconceived notion of what constitutes "ideal." When other people's qualities or traits don't suit us, we try to mask them out or paint them over. But it never works. We can't make others conform to our image of what they *should* be. Furthermore, we can't become what they wish we were. Sooner or later we discover each other's flaws, and they become the first basis of disappointment and disagreement between us.

When we really have the makings of a relationship, however, we are able to get past our petty disappointments and put them in perspective. With increasing trust and devotion, we can lift off our mask and reveal ourselves completely, believing we will be accepted.

Our little problems and shortcomings might even be valued. After all, a slight imperfection in a piece of art is what makes it unique, and we value it all the more highly because it is one of a kind. We all are one of a kind, and our failings are as much a part of us as our fine points.

So remember—your first disagreement is not the end of the world: it may just mean you're discovering each other. Look hard. Each of you may find in the other a true work of art.

her letter

Dear . . .

Well, now you know I'm not all I'm cracked up to be. I'm not always cool and collected. Neither am I always sweet and gentle. I could excuse myself by saying that it was very hot and the trip was long and uncomfortable with no air conditioning. I could add that you had promised to fix the air conditioner last week and that you didn't. You also said that you had checked our reser-vations and it turned out you hadn't.

I now know you aren't as organized as you seem. And now that I've thought it over—what a relief! You don't know how happy it makes me to know you're not perfect. I thought you had no flaws. It was downright scary. I figured if you were so perfect, you'd never accept me. Pretty soon, I feared, you'd discover a whole raft of my faults and cast me to the winds. I have plenty but I'm not going to list them. They'll announce themselves soon enough.

Let's look at the truth. We had a great time once we got a room—and a shower. It's a lovely inn, a beautiful town. I'm sorry we wasted so much time feuding before we got there. Here's to knowing you better and to our next trip.

Love,
Linda

P.S. | When you write after your first disagreement:

Do put the disagreement in perspective. It's neither the end of the world nor of your relationship.

Do acknowledge that the other person not only has a right to their own opinions but that you appreciate their independence.

Do state that the disagreement in no way diminishes your love.

Don't rehash the disagreement and don't stir the ashes. Leave it alone and the fire will burn itself out.

Don't overdo the apology stuff. If you make too big a deal out of it, it will become a big deal. 'Nuff said.

After the First Argument

Things that are past, it is needless to blame.
—Confucius, *Analects*

He that is slow to anger is better than the mighty.
—Proverbs 16:18

his feelings

Everything was going along so perfectly. You were in seventh heaven, truly walking on air. Then, almost out of nowhere, you had your first argument. Crestfallen, you've begun to question the entire relationship.

Step back a minute and think. Every couple that's ever existed has had arguments. It's all part of living. It's all part of loving. Why are some couples better able to survive an occasional argument than others? They've learned that an argument can actually be a constructive force which strengthens their relationship—providing they've learned *how* to argue.

153

Arguments rarely just happen. Rather, somewhat like volcanoes, they are the result of pressures built up over time. Regular communication acts as a safety valve to relieve those pressures. Absent that, eruptions are bound to occur. Not to worry, as Grandma used to say. A healthy argument provides an opportunity for each partner to help the other better understand those things in the relationship that have been generating pressure. Better understanding—that's the constructive purpose of an argument. Better understanding leads to conflict resolution which, in turn, leads to a happier relationship.

But how to achieve better understanding in the throes of an argument, you ask. There are several ways. Stick to the point of the disagreement. Don't discuss irrelevancies and don't rehash past arguments. Listen to what your partner is saying. When you speak, make your point without invective—neither be insulting nor attack your partner's attributes or characteristics over which they have no control. Avoid foul language. Don't exaggerate and try not to shout. After all, this is someone you supposedly truly care for. The goal is not to "win"—a relationship is not a debating society or a courtroom. The goal is to help the other person understand why you are so upset or angry. If they understand, there is a chance for improvement. If you force them to be defensive, all of your energies will be self-defeating. Nothing will be accomplished.

Oh, but I will have gotten it out of my system, you say. At what price? Weakening you relationship or, perhaps, even ending it. If you learn nothing else from this book, learn that once the harsh word is written or spoken it cannot be taken back. You can pull out a misplaced nail but the hole will remain.

Remember, you can be candid, honest and forthright. You can make your point and express yourself forcefully and effectively—without *attacking* the other person. If you must "fight"—and all couples since Adam and Eve have—fight fair. That's the basic rule.

In our household we always accepted, as a perfectly reasonable outcome of an argument and after each of us had had our say, the statement, "Well, we disagree." Not every conflict can be resolved. Each of us is an individual and perfection is simply an ideal.

Ah, but what now? The argument is spent. Let it rest. Move on to other things. And, then, find an opportunity to let your loved one know that you still care, that you're still there.

So how come I have so much to say about arguments? Because once upon a time I didn't fight fair and once upon a time I thought I could apologize for words that should never have been spoken and all would be forgiven. And once upon a time. . . I lost her.

I should have written her the following letter. Actually, I should have known better.

his Letter

Dearest . . .

If we never have another argument, it will be too soon for me. Yes, I know that arguments, like thunderstorms, are part of life. Thunderstorms, with all their fury, ultimately pass and arguments end. Sometimes a storm does real harm but sometimes the noise and the wind mean nothing while the rain replenishes the soil and makes things grow anew.

I hope our storm didn't do any permanent harm. I am not proud of my part in that argument for I said things in the heat of the moment I clearly did not mean and I'm ashamed of that. But, through it all, I heard what you said and this morning I understand more clearly than before why you were so upset. I believe you understand why I was. So maybe some good will come out of it and we, too, will grow anew.

I want you to know that at no time, even during those awful moments, did I ever doubt my love for you or, truly, yours for me.

If I cared less, the argument would have meant, and hurt, less. But I don't care less, I care more—each passing day I genuinely care more.

I've still got some thinking to do but I just had to write and say how much, how very much, I love you and how sorry I am for my part in it all.

Now let's put it behind us. We have some rebuilding to do. Let's make what we've learned work for us so we'll be stronger than before.

We'll try and we'll succeed. Loving each other as we do, we'll succeed.

Sid

hER FEELINGS

If you never argue, you're either a saint, a fool, or both. You also may be carrying a lot of resentment inside. Remember that fateful line on your report card from first, second, and third grade? "Gets along well with peers." I always got a perfect score on that one. I never told the teacher that Freddie threatened to bury my head in the sandbox if I didn't surrender my snack. I gave Janie my new pencil and took her stubby one in return. I wanted Janie to invite me home to play. I lost a lot of Ring-Dings and apples and when I finally was invited to Janie's house, I didn't have much fun.

In my house, we didn't argue. When my sister and I squabbled, we were told to go to our rooms and not to come out until we could get along. Before going to bed, we had to kiss and make up. "Don't let the sun set on your anger," we were told. To this day, we still find it hard to acknowledge what we're really feeling and often have a lot of making up to do.

If you are similarly conditioned not to fight, your first argument with your partner may seem devastating. But you are no longer in grade school and you are *not* in a popularity contest. No more report cards, either.

It's time to change your attitude. You can't get back your Ring-Ding or whatever you lost in childhood. But you may keep your lover. In fact, he's probably just as upset as you are.

Nonfighters or poor fighters must learn some rules.

Rule 1: Speak up! But speak up properly. Don't bring all the leftover ammunition you never used in the past into the present skirmish. Your partner is your opponent for the moment, not your enemy. You want negotiation, not war.

Rule 2: Stick to the issue. Don't bring up other grievances.

Rule 3: Say what you mean. Nonfighters often hope, foolishly, that others will guess what they are feeling. They can't. It won't happen. As a nonfighter, you seldom say what you really mean and you suspect that others do the same. You invest their words with all sort of hidden messages. You must learn to clarify what you're feeling and express it in plain English. If you're not sure of what he's really saying, ask. You want communication, not a guessing game.

Rule 4: Fight fair. This is hard for fighters and nonfighters alike. It means not hitting below the belt—not making it personal. It means not blaming or accusing, which will only polarize your positions, calling up defensiveness and more hostility.

Rule 5: Apologize if and when needed. It takes two to quarrel, whether actively or passively. If you think that love means you never have to say you're sorry, you've got a long search for love ahead of you.

Rule 6: Don't carry a grudge. Once your argument is talked out, let it go. You may have reached only a compromise or a truce. You'll have other arguments over other issues, maybe even the same issue. Disagreement is part of life, part of the blending of two different, changing selves. Don't hold on to your anger. Look for ways to build your love and overcome your differences.

her Letter

Dear . . .

I'm a bad "fighter," and you know it. You're a bad fighter too. I call you names and you call me names. I accuse and you accuse. You yell. I sulk. Really great for clearing the air, isn't it? We fuss, we fume, but we patch it up and bury it. We never resolve anything.

Last night, we went ten rounds and we still didn't resolve anything. I started it. You hadn't done anything other than what you usually do—forget the clock. You were two hours late but didn't see why it should be a big deal. After all, we hadn't planned anything special. I didn't tell you that I had passed up a chance to see an old friend because I was expecting you. Instead I let you have it with every grievance I've collected over the years. I started with your lateness in particular and worked up to your complete lack of caring for me or my life and your total disregard for any of my needs. I was blaming you for any time anyone ever made me wait, for every opportunity I ever let pass. You accused me of being an ingrate and a jailer.

Neither one of us was right. I don't really believe you disregard me or aren't concerned about me. How could I? You show your concern for me every day. You take time from your own work to help me with mine. You have made midnight runs to deliver my work for me. You have helped me with mailings, with presentations, with proposals. So I guess I deserved the "ingrate" label.

Why did I make such a big fuss over two hours and why did it become so important last night? It's because this has become a pattern between us and I've been helping it continue. You're always late because a crazy schedule is habitual with you. You have a lot of interruptions. Colleagues and students stop you in the hall. You have a lot of unexpected phone calls. People break appointments and you have to work them in next week, next month.

The changes wreak havoc with your own life. I know you'd like to have a more predictable life. You've said so often enough. But I fell into the pattern because it suited my own craziness. I don't have fixed hours, and I liked having time stay flexible. So what if we didn't get where we were going at the right time or on the right day. There was always another place, another day. It wasn't until the changes started wreaking havoc with my own life that I recognized the crazy pattern. Lately we can't even seem to take a shower or take out the garbage without consulting our appointment books. Let's face it. We've got a problem.

What I didn't deserve was the name of jailer. I don't ask you for minute-to-minute bulletins of your whereabouts. And I don't insist that you drop what you're doing or change your plans in order to rush home by six o'clock. Here's what I do want: a call from you if our plans together have to be changed because your schedule has changed. And I want to be notified as soon as possible. That's not asking any more than your dentist would ask. It's a simple courtesy. I can do a lot with a sudden free hour, a suddenly free afternoon. I can finish a job, run some errands, visit a friend.

Let's have a rematch and let's agree to two conditions: we'll stick to the issue and we won't push anything under the rug. With a little careful planning, maybe we can settle this and have some time left over for fun.

Love,
Linda

P.S. When you write your letter after your first argument:

Do state how badly you feel.

Do put the argument into perspective.

Do note how important the relationship is to you and that you want it to continue and grow.

Don't rehash the argument.

Don't try to score "points" in writing you failed to score orally.

Don't try to "win." If you do, you'll lose.

What I Need in Our Relationship

Let there be truth between us two forevermore.
—Ralph Waldo Emerson, "Behavior"

ḣer ꝼeeliꝿgs

As children, if we're lucky, we get our needs met just by existing. We're hungry: food appears We're cold: blankets and warm, comforting arms enfold us. We're scared: a soothing voice croons to us. How wonderful if our adult needs were met so quickly, easily, and fully. Actually, it would be even more wonderful if our needs stayed so simple and were communicated and understood without effort. But they don't and they're not. Instead they become increasingly more complicated and the persons we want most to fill them may feel no obligation or need to do so. Most of us have some leftover childhood needs that can never be filled—only lived with and, we hope, outgrown.

Distinguishing between the needs we have a hope of fulfilling, the ones we have a right to expect to be met, and the ones that probably never will be met is a difficult task. We learn to furnish ourselves with food and shelter and to achieve a reasonable measure of security. In social and work situations we learn to work out compromises or negotiate to achieve a satisfactory atmosphere or to obtain what we perceive as our just compensation. If we don't, we move on to other friends and other jobs.

Negotiating the atmosphere of and meeting mutual needs in a love relationship can be trickier. More than friendship is involved. You and your lover are not boss and employee. Still, you have a contract: You hope to build a future together. The stakes in your relationship are higher than those of friendship or any other work. For work it is, and ongoing. The tough job of communicating, understanding, and internalizing each other's needs that is vital to the progress of your relationship begins when it does. If the work stops, the relationship usually stops too.

Negotiating the basic conditions of your relationship—how to divvy up chores, how and with whom to spend your leisure time— may be pretty simple. Even if you differ drastically in personal habits, interests, and tastes, you can work out effective compromises and either overcome or agree to ignore what you can't change. Meeting each other's emotional needs is not so simple. Talking it out may not help, even if you pick a special time and place to talk. The emotions themselves get in the way, clogging up the airwaves, and you end up "speaking in code," rehashing old arguments, and never saying what you mean to say. When he is half an hour late and doesn't call, you may feel threatened for reasons that have little or nothing to do with him or the present. Lateness to you means abandonment, means broken promises, means insecurity—all connected with your past. But you don't articulate this. You don't even try. Instead, you attack: "You're late! And I bet you forgot to get the car serviced." On the defensive, and feeling the attack, he responds: "I called you this afternoon. Do I have to check in every hour on the hour? And what do I look like? The handyman?"

Many couples repeat such frustrating exchanges over and over, never verbalizing their real feelings. Other couples don't verbalize their needs at all. They may expect the partner to sense their needs and emotions as a loving mother would. They may want to avoid confrontation. They may be used to having needs ignored or believe that they will be perceived as overly demanding. Whatever the reasons, they remain quiet. None of these behavior patterns are conducive to understanding and growth.

If any or all of these things are operative in your relationship, a letter may help you overcome them and express yourself fully to your partner. The act of putting pen to paper is freeing. It's not chiseled in stone. You can reword and rework it until you have said everything you really want to say.

---

hER LETTER

Dear . . .

What I need most in our relationship is unqualified security. I know you can't provide it. Nobody could. This need stems from my past; I've never felt secure. Like most people, I have an old attic in my head where I keep unmet needs and unresolved issues left over from the past. The biggest piece of furniture up there is my Insecurity Bureau. It's full of broken promises, rejection, and lies.

What I need in our relationship is a feeling of security, and that feeling is growing stronger with every day of our relationship. I guess I never will get the Insecurity Bureau out of my attic. Like many other people, I'm attached to old junk. But I'm going to try to keep away from the attic. Our relationship has put new

*furniture in my life. It's bright, modern, and clean. I have a new
bureau now. Its top drawer is filled with the support and love
you've given me. I have hope that the other drawers will fill up
with good things too.*

Love,
Linda

P.S. | When you tell your beloved what you need in your relationship:

Do be sure your expectations are reasonable. If you need someone by your side every minute in order not to feel alone, if you need daily reassurance that you are desirable and loved, you need a therapist, not a relationship.

Do leave the door open for a response. If you accuse or blame, your partner may only respond by attacking.

Don't be afraid to say what you are feeling. Stick to your feelings. Your partner may not even realize that his or her actions or manner affects you in the way it does or that you are lacking anything in your relationship.

Don't use code. Be specific. If you feel your partner is inattentive, state how and why—and what it means to you. If you aren't consulted before a decision is made, don't accuse your partner of having contempt for you—say you want to participate. If you are a woman and think your partner is not responsive to your lovemaking overtures, don't claim a lack of sensibility. Say you'd like to be the instigator at times. Use plain English. Make your message unmistakable.

You Hurt Me

. . . pain clings cruelly to us.
    —John Keats, "Endymion"

There is weeping in my heart . . .
    —Paul Verlaine, *Romances sans paroles*

his feelings

It is important to "speak up" when you have been hurt by the other person in your relationship. Failure to do so, bravely suffering in silence, accomplishes nothing. There are no rewards on earth for martyrdom. Unless you express your feelings, there is no way your partner will know them. Knowledge is, in this as in all things, the first step toward understanding.

If you lock those hurt feelings inside, become sullen and withdrawn or inexplicably angry, it's as if you are saying to your friend, "I'm upset. Guess why?" It's a game and game-playing destroys relationships. Besides, if that hurt is kept inside it will continue to eat at you and, ultimately, turn to anger.

No, far better to tell her what you think she did wrong and why it hurt you. If she truly cares for you, she'll take what you say seriously and the hurt may not be repeated.

Make sure, of course, that you are not overreacting to a perceived as opposed to a genuine slight, leave room for the very real possibility that her actions were unintentional and, once again, remember you are not striking back - you are explaining. Express yourself candidly but minimize hostility and maximize tenderness.

his Letter

Dear . . .

Last week we had an argument. We differed strongly, expressed our opinions fully, things got "hot" for a while and then cooled down. Shit happens. Neither of us expected smooth sailing all the way. In fact, our ability to weather storms is one of the strengths of our relationship.

But last night at dinner and in the presence of our best friends, you felt obliged to air the "dirty laundry." I kept silent then— partially out of surprise, largely because I simply didn't know how to respond. Now I do.

You hurt me. I can't believe you wanted to and I'm sure you're sorry. At least that's what I choose to believe. But you hurt me nonetheless and I had to let you know how I felt—both for my respect and yours.

If there was something more about the argument you wanted to say, you should have said it to me. I would have listened. I may not have agreed, but I surely would have listened. But to have done so in public was a lack of grace and good form that is atypical of you. You are a kind, sympathetic and well-mannered person. Therefore, your conduct last night was all the more incomprehensible.

It just can't happen again. Either I am important to you, at least important enough to be extended the same courtesy and consideration you'd give a casual acquaintance, or I don't belong in your life. Just because we have weathered other storms doesn't mean we aren't capable of capsizing.

We're supposed to love each other for better or worse. I'll tell you—it's a lot easier to love you for better . . .
                                        Sid

her feelings

That's it. THE END. No one who loved you could have hurt you the way he did. And those things he said. He knows just what words to say to cut you most. Actually, only those who know you, those who love you, *can* cut you deeply. If a stranger curses you on the street, you are not affected. Uncomfortable maybe, and angry for a moment. But you realize you are being cursed at by a nut, that you are a momentary and impersonal target.

As lovers, however, we slowly learn each other's vulnerable spots, the delicate places we want no one to tread on, the soft underbellies. In *The Once and Future King (Part 1: The Sword and the Stone)*, T.H. White describes young King Arthur's early training. Merlyn transforms Art into various animals so that he can experience their feelings and existences. As a fierce badger, Art encounters a hedgehog who has curled itself in a tight ball, its spiky spines protruding as protection.

"Uncurl!" orders Art.

"Please doant ask 'un to uncurl," replies the trembling urchin. "All's fear in love and war . . . ." The urchin then describes badgers: ". . . don't they fair give you a nip without a-noticin' of it? . . . . Get in their way for a moment and without nary wicked intention and 'tis snip, snap, just like that . . . and then where are you? . . .and they comes about and asks [you] to uncurl."

Wisely, the hedgehog does not uncurl, and young Art doesn't insist. Lovers do uncurl, perhaps wisely. Trust and intimacy increases with revelation. But so does vulnerability. And with nary truly wicked intention, it's hard not to use weapons you know will hurt when you fight. If you're poorly coordinated and he calls you a klutz, he's struck a low blow. If in turn, you know he's sensitive about a receding hairline, you're not fighting fair if you call him Telly.

These blows are low, but they're not killers. The problem is that once you start, stopping isn't easy. Neither is turning the other cheek. After all, who wants to be hit on both? Instead, the temptation is to escalate. And the more bruising the words exchanged, the longer and more hurtfully they echo.

Some things, such as physical abuse or continuing breach of trust, can't be forgiven. Words, though, even if they cannot be recalled, usually can be forgiven. Even if you believe that you are the injured party, ask yourself what your role has been in the quarrel. Cool off. Then use words to mend the gulf between you: a letter. When you write it, don't escalate further by accusing or blaming. Acknowledge your role. Set new boundaries if need be. And add a hefty helping of love.

ḥER LETTER

Dear . . .

Last night I would have driven home alone, but I didn't want to leave you stranded. By the end of the evening I was sorry I hadn't.

What a miserable ride we had. We yelled a lot, and we said a lot of ugly things to each other. I have to tell you what I'm feeling now that I've had some time to think it over.

I shouldn't have gone in the first place. I knew she would be there and that you were bound to talk to each other. After all, you were together for two years. What I didn't expect was for you to leave me standing in the hall as soon as you saw her. I felt humiliated. I didn't know anyone there, and you didn't even take time to introduce me.

You kept saying that I was jealous. You're right—to a degree. I had some green flashes in front of my eyes. But I'm not suspicious or mistrustful. Those words hurt and I think you were unfair. The simple truth is this: you were rude. Usually your manners are good but last night they were bad. I found it hard to reconcile your behavior with the idea that you care for me.

I'm not excusing my own bad manners. I shouldn't have made accusations I knew were false. We called each other a lot of names, none of them accurate. Anger and defensiveness got us nowhere, except unhappier, if that's possible, than we already were.

You hurt me, but I'm sure you didn't do it with intent. Let's put last night behind us and find where we left our manners.

Love,
Linda

P.S. | When you express your hurt:

Do consider whether the hurt was genuine and whether you were in any way at fault.

Do be specific. It's important that you let your partner know exactly what was done that hurt you.

Do explain why you were hurt.

Do explain what a continuation of that conduct must eventually mean for your relationship.

Do let your partner know what you expect in the future.

Do let it be known that you still care for him or her and that you understand we all make mistakes and we all have the capacity to grow.

Don't hurt back. Two wrongs never make a right.

Don't threaten. It may work temporarily but in the long run it is counterproductive.

I'm So Sorry . . . Please Forgive Me

Love is blind; friendship closes its eyes.
—French proverb

his feelings

"You ou always hurt the one you love, the one you shouldn't hurt at all," sang the Mills Brothers. It's true, it's unfortunate, but it's understandable. When someone is in love, they are particularly vulnerable to the actions and reactions, to the moods, even to the facial expressions of the one they love. I think it's because when someone is so very happy, they don't want anything to endanger that happiness. Thus, like Chicken Little, if an acorn drops they fear the sky is falling.

So, frequently without meaning to, we do something or say

something that hurts the one we love, "the one you shouldn't hurt at all." Sometimes we just forget that loved ones have to be treated with an extra measure of consideration. Just like the Japanese removing their shoes before entering a traditional home, something of our other self, our outside world self, should be cast aside when we enter the presence of our beloved. There is wisdom in that old bit of advice, "Don't bring the office home." (At least don't bring your office self home.)

It's also the case that on occasion we test our relationships. We may test them to see how much freedom and independence we still have. Sometimes we engage in a test of wills—a power struggle to determine who "controls" the relationship. If we push too hard, someone's bound to get hurt.

Whether through inadvertence, inattention or brusqueness, it is true our words or actions can be hurtful. Whenever that's the case, an apology is due. You should no more allow a hurt to remain unattended than you'd allow a wound to go without treatment. Hurts are wounds and unless you do whatever is reasonably necessary to help them heal, they will fester.

When I've hurt someone I want to make sure they know how sorry I feel. I tend to tell them face to face but frequently I follow up with a letter.

ḣis Leccer

Dearest . . .

You have to know that I'd die before consciously hurting you. You are the best thing that's ever happened to me. Not a day passes that I don't say a prayer of thanksgiving because you came into my life. Only if you understand that can you possibly understand how truly sorry I am for the pain I caused you.

I know that sometimes I speak without thinking or act without thinking. But not often or you wouldn't care for me the way I know you do.

There is a saving grace. Imperfect as I may be, I know that God's not finished with me yet. With his help, tomorrow I'll be a better guy than I am today. With His help—and with yours.

Please forgive me. I define myself by my reflection in your eyes. This morning I need to see forgiveness there.

Sid

ħER FEELIŊGS

Love will tolerate a lot of stress and strain, but it won't tolerate *abuse*. Unfortunately, it's easy for lovers to abuse each other. That's because you can't *be* lovers without exposing your tender spots. So if your lover wants to hurt you, he knows where to hit. If you want to hurt him, you know where to hit too. During the course of a heated argument it's tempting to make use of the secrets with which you've been trusted, but you shouldn't. You shouldn't strike your lover in his weak spots and he shouldn't strike you in yours.

To strike someone in a weak spot he's shown you *is* abuse—definitely. One who does this takes the trust he's been given and uses it for a wrongful purpose. He's like the public official who steals from the treasury he's supposed to guard. We say that such an official has *abused* the public trust. Similarly if, in the course of a fight with your partner, you have deliberately hit where it hurts, you have abused him and you should apologize.

Neglect is also a form of abuse. Consider the man who is careful to be courteous, polite and attentive to those he works with but who, in the presence of his partner, forgets his manners —his best colors. He defends himself, of course, with thoughts like these: "Why should I put on an act at home? Who needs to pretend among one's own? My family *knows* how much I value them."

Nothing could be more wrong. Love, like any living thing, thrives on attention, acknowledgment, appreciation, consideration, and courtesy. But we all forget, and most of us do abuse others at times. When we do, though, we should be sorry. Furthermore, we ought to say so.

ḢER LETTER

Dear . . .

What's the matter with me? I'm so sorry. I have been taking you for granted or for granite. You are so self-contained and even-tempered that I think of you as a rock, a pillar on which I can lean. I forget your feelings. I have been taking advantage of your good nature.

I spend a lot of time thanking people throughout the day. I thank the telephone operator and the store clerk. I thank the service station attendant. I thank the paper boy and the repair man. I almost never thank you and there are so many things I have to thank you for.

You are my greatest admirer; you overlook my faults and praise my accomplishments, instilling me with confidence. You are my playmate for parties and vacations and yet you're always there to help me clean up anything from spilled milk to spilled tears. You are my abiding comfort and love.

You are always willing to listen to me. More than that, you hear what I say and respond. I don't always give you the same consideration. I cut you off rudely yesterday when you wanted to talk because I didn't want to stop watching the movie. You looked hurt, but I let it slide. Later, watching you sleep, I thought about what I had done. I realized it wasn't the first time I had seen that look in your eyes.

I never want to see that look again and know that I am responsible for it. I can't cancel out yesterday or any of the hurt I've caused you before, but I can try to remain aware every day of all that you mean to me and to return in greater measure all that you give to me. Please forgive me for my carelessness and neglect.

Love,
Linda

P.S. When you write to say you're sorry:

Do be genuinely sorry. Sincerity and contrition are at the heart of a true apology.

Do accept responsibility for your own conduct.

Do let the other person know that you understand why what you did was wrong.

Do make it clear that the hurt you caused has caused you hurt.

Do, definitely do, explain that you have no intention of repeating the hurtful conduct.

Don't grovel. You are an adult apologizing to an adult.

Don't, under any circumstances, try to excuse your misconduct.

I Think of You Often

All thoughts, all passions, all delights,
Whatever stirs this mortal frame
All are but ministers of Love
And feed his sacred flame.
—Samuel Taylor Coleridge, "Love"

his feelings

otevery love letter need express undying ardor. In fact, such a series of missives would be suspect. "Methinks the [person] protesteth too much."

Sometimes it is enough simply to let another know they are in your thoughts.

his Letter

Dear . . .

This morning as I stood by the picture window watching the sun slowly make its way up and over the horizon, I thought of you.

At midday strolling through the park admiring the budding blossoms, I thought of you.

During a meeting, I smiled recalling something you said last weekend; driving home I found myself humming our song.

Now, at day's end, I close my eyes and try to imagine what you are doing this very moment.

The thought of you is woven throughout my day. You have become the theme of my existence. I'd have it no other way.

Until remembrance becomes presence and thought reality. . .

Sid

her feelings

Valuable assets need attention. Most people get their cars tuned up frequently. A car is an important asset and a big investment. Regular maintenance is necessary to keep running smoothly. An apartment or home is an even greater asset, a bigger investment, and one that requires even greater attention to upkeep. We are willing to pay attention. We accept these facts. We even insure our assets. We want to protect them.

Protection pays off. The car runs well. The home is comfortable and pleasant. But what if we didn't pay such close attention? What if we ignored the first little nick in the car's paint, a pulled thread in the living room carpet. We wouldn't be very surprised if the nick became a rust spot, if the carpet began to unravel.

Your relationship is certainly a vital asset, one you want to protect. But once it is established and familiar, and as long as it is running smoothly, it's easy to take for granted. You may not pay such close attention to it anymore. You may not notice little nicks in its surface, a fraying of its edges. Don't let it happen. Give your relationship regularly scheduled maintenance, love tuneups. Insure your love with a little encouragement, a bit of praise, a word of affection, a hug, a touch, a small surprise, a letter. These premiums are not expensive. And don't wait for a birthday, an anniversary. Anytime will do.

ђER LETTER

Dear . . .

When things are difficult for me, I think of you. I know that when I see you, you will discuss the problems. You'll listen carefully and help me see them clearly. With that in mind, I feel calmer right away. I can ride it out. My temper and emotions don't rule me any more, and my life is much smoother in every aspect. You're largely responsible for that.

When things are going great, I think of you. I want you to be the first to know of some achievement of mine, a new client or prospect, a success. I know that you will be as happy about it as I am.

I think of you often. I picture you at your computer, fingers flying. I see you pacing, head down, hands held behind you, as you ponder your next page or project. I see you seated at the piano, towel around your waist, hair dripping wet. "I've got it. The last line!" You want it on paper, right now.

I think of you many times a day, and all my thoughts are warm. The patina of my love for you is as shiny and bright as it was when we first met. Yet I seldom tell you of my thoughts or of all you mean to me in every moment of our life.

I thought it was about time I told you. I want it on paper, right now.

With all my love,
Linda

P.S.	When you write to tell someone they are often in your thoughts:
	Do tell them what it means to you to have them in your thoughts.
	Do express how good thinking of them makes you feel.
	Don't write this letter unless the thoughts are pleasant. None of this, "I think of you often and to tell you the truth . . ."

How I Miss You

Carrier of love and sympathy, messenger of friendship,
consoler of the lonely, servant of the scattered family . . .
—Inscriptions for the East
and West Pavilions, Post Office,
Washington, D.C.

his feelings

L onging isn't loving but it is a signpost along the way. You know you really care about someone when, even though you lead a full life, their absence hurts, when you miss them, when you wish they were with you.

"I've grown accustomed to her face," Professor Higgins sang to Eliza Doolittle. But it's more than just familiarity. There are some people whose mere presence adds to the quality of our life. We are, quite simply, happier when they are with us—more fulfilled and complete. It may not be definable but it is felt.

If I find myself noticing with regularity that she's not there, when I start to say something to her that she can't hear, if her absence means the house is empty and so am I, I know for sure she has become a part of my life. I like to let her know she is missed because sometimes I think she wonders just how much she continues to mean to me and whether, since we live so far apart, the maxim "out of sight, out of mind" applies. I want her to understand that in reality she's more than missed—she's needed.

Last weekend the woman to whom I wrote the letter in Chapter 21 ("I Love You") came down from Montreal to visit for the Easter holiday weekend. For the last few days since she returned home, busy as I have been with other things, there has been a dull ache in my heart and I have been walking around in a bit of a fog. Miss her? I long for her! And I long for her because I do love her so.

I really ought to tell her. She deserves to know.

---

his Letter

Dearest . . .

The house is so still. I tread ever so softly from room to room lest I disturb last week's memories.

There you are at the breakfast table bundled in my Joseph's robe, cute beyond all measure. And again in the living room with the Times spread out before you. Hello, is that you on the terrace angling to obtain "the" perfect picture of the Tappan Zee Bridge swooping across the Hudson? Once more, you're in the den poking among my books and tapes.

Nor is the village without your presence. Walking up North Broadway today I saw us jogging there and laughed aloud at the remembrance of a fifty-year-old man trying to pretend to his meaningfully younger friend that, no, he wasn't winded. From every shop window your image is reflected; each quaint garden recalls your praise.

I was in the city yesterday and you were with me. Several times I went out of my way to show you again sights we had seen together when you were here. There are, you know, places that henceforth will belong only to us: a vest-pocket park, a side street, a café. Fortunately, there are those places we did not get to visit. A moment's respite from your memory except that passing them I remember you again.

It's not as if we haven't talked. I've enjoyed a wonderful conversation with you all week. Would that you had been here to respond. . .

It's a good thing that I do not miss you—or how could I function at all? A good thing, indeed.

Once again I am half until you return and make me whole.

Sid

bER fEELINGS

Separation is difficult, but most of us learn to deal with it. Think about little children. They don't quite understand that separation is temporary. When their parents go out for an evening, they are bereft. Their eyes are bright with tears as a babysitter takes charge of their care. On the first day of kindergarten, four- and five-year-olds clutch frantically at their mothers' legs when the big yellow bus approaches.

Yet toddlers are usually peacefully asleep when parents *come home* from an evening out. Kindergartners are smug and satisfied when they take the yellow bus *home* at the end of the day, proudly displaying their first fingerpainting suitable for hanging on the refrigerator. Slowly, independence evolves. Kids learn that they can survive separation and that people do come back.

The truth is that each of us is a separate being, and if we develop normally (more or less), we come to accept that fact (more or less). With the very first breath we take when we wriggle out of the womb, we are biologically separate from every other being on earth, and that's the way we stay, all our lives.

But separate does not mean alone. When we love, healthily and freely, we can usually expect someone to *meet* our yellow bus if we need them to. And, depending on the circumstances, we can usually expect the same someone to come home at the end of the day, the week, or the month. Separation is hard and it always will be. But when it has you down, review the lesson you learned as a child: separation is natural, and it's temporary.

ḣer Leccer

Dear . . .

I miss you very much. I haven't had much time to be lonely though. You'll be pleased to see what I have accomplished since you've been gone. I finally painted some pictures I wanted to frame.

When you first told me how long you would be gone, I was very unhappy. Three months! And so far away. For a while I couldn't imagine what I would do with myself. All those mornings, all those nights alone. But five weeks have already passed. My new course starts tomorrow night. Alison suggested that she might be interested in a few of my pictures. If that doesn't happen, I'll still have them when you get back. Maybe you'd like one or two for your walls at home.

And speaking of home, I'll be happy to see you back here. I'll meet you at the airport. You should have no trouble picking me out of the crowd. I'll be wearing a raincoat (with nothing underneath). I don't think anyone else will be dressed that way. After all, honey, it never rains in Southern California. Hurry home.

Love,
Linda

P.S. | When you write to say "I miss you":

Do tell *why*—what it is about your loved one you cherish when he or she is with you and miss when they are not.

Do tell what it means to you to have your loved one with you and what it means to you when they are gone—express your feelings.

Do invite your loved one to return soon. Why suffer?

Don't say, "I miss you," if you do not mean it. Boomerangs return.

How Did We Let This Happen?

And ruined love, when it is built anew,
Grows fairer than at first, more strong, far greater . . .
—Shakespeare, Sonnet 19

Come back! Come back! dearest friend! . . .
I swear to you I shall henceforth be kind . . .
—Arthur Rimbaud, letter to Paul Verlaine

his feelings

One moment you're a couple, the next you're not. "How did we let this happen?"

I've asked that question of myself a number of times. Almost always the answer comes back: we didn't communicate enough. If only I had told her . . . Why didn't she say? . . . I thought we had agreed to . . . No matter what the actual issues are that divide a couple, the failure to discuss them sufficiently is almost always the actual cause of the schism.

"Let this happen." That's the key. We let bad things happen in our relationships by not communicating enough. How many times in my life I wished I could roll back the clock a day, an hour, just five minutes so I could tell her how I really felt. If wishes were fishes, no man would go hungry.

What to do? Start communicating. It is never too late to make the effort. Right now write now.

---

his Letter

Dearest . . .

If someone had told us just a while ago that we would no longer be together, neither of us would have believed it. Our days were magical, our nights mystical, and the golden chains of love that bound us together were so entwined we thought they'd never break. Was it all but a dream? If so, I wish we had never awakened. If those were the happiest times of my life, these are the unhappiest. Living without you is barely living at all.

What happened and why? That question haunts me. It's almost all I've thought about since we broke up. Perhaps we took each other for granted. That's easy to do when things are going well. But love is like a garden that needs careful tending. I know that now.

We assumed too much and communicated too little. Expected too much and gave too little. And so everything we had together began to unravel until the very fabric of our relationship was in shreds.

Thomas Wolfe said you can't go home again. I think he was wrong. Only by leaving home do you really begin to appreciate it. Never had I appreciated your love as much as when I had lost it. Never had I appreciated what we had together as I did when we no longer had it.

The fault lies not in our stars but in ourselves, wrote Shakespeare. What happened to us was clearly our fault and not our destiny. Yet what can be broken or torn can also be fixed or mended. I believe that our lives are in our own hands. It's up to us to make of it what we will. I still want to make my life with you. I still want you to make yours with me.

This time we'll make it work because this time we'll work at it together. That's what people who love each other should do. And deep in my heart I know we still do love each other. If I know anything in life, I know that.

Sid

her feelings

Something's wrong in Paradise. You don't know exactly what it is or why it happened. You're not even sure when it began. All you know is that you became dissatisfied or unhappy. He seemed even more so. You talked it over—and over and over. You made "contracts" with each other: "I won't be late if you'll promise to control your temper." "I'll agree not to criticize you in public if you'll stop criticizing my friends." But the contracts didn't really hold, or didn't address the real problems or the number of problems between you. Now you can't seem to be together for two hours before you are enmeshed in tension and bickering.

How do we reach such a state—with the shiny gloss of our love dulled, deadened, abraded? No relationship is immune to the possibility of infidelity or gross abuse of trust. But recent studies indicate that many partners remain monogamous through long relationships and marriages. What's more, a good union can surmount great lapses and become even stronger.

It is not one destructive act but a succession of acts of both commission and omission that erode and destroy a union. As we become more and more sure of our partner's love, we relax into it. We neglect to praise or to thank. We no longer enthuse over the qualities that drew us to each other. We become impatient, intolerant. The marvelous is familiar, mundane, and no longer so appreciated. The feeling of privilege has become a feeling of entitlement. When we have reached such a state of dissatisfaction, we are likely to blame our partner for it: *They* have changed. *They* haven't lived up to our expectations. *They* don't care enough about us. Actually, they probably haven't changed much, and no person can fill all our expectations. And your partner probably does care, even greatly, and is as bewildered as you are at the present state of affairs.

What to do? Start all over? A new partner, the right partner? The ideal? If you find him, let me know. Let all of us know. We won't hold our collective breath, though. We think you are doomed to a long and unsuccessful hunt. Instead, we suggest working (very hard) on your present relationship. Recapture your first feelings, remember what attracted you in the beginning stages of your love, consider the qualities that you still admire and respect in your partner. Make a list. Include the negative qualities. Now make a list of your own good and bad qualities. Ask yourself (and answer yourself honestly) whether you manifest your best self in your relationship. You may convict yourself of deficiencies as great as those you perceive in your partner—or greater. Now make a "New Life" resolution. You don't have to say it out loud or put it on paper. Your resolution is simple: "Accentuate the positive." When you write your letter, don't dwell on the past. Don't bury him in it with "If only you had done this" and "Why didn't you do that?" Acknowledge the present only briefly. He's as well aware of it as you are. Then let him know not what you miss in him, but what you value in him. Assure him of the depth of your feeling and of its endurance.

her Letter

Dear . . .

I'm sorry. I'm sorry for my part in what happened and what's been happening. I'm even sorrier that we didn't keep it just between us. I'd give a lot to erase the bad words and bad feelings, most of all the things I said that Friday. When my sister and I used to fight, my mother would say, "Your tongue's tied in the middle and loose at both ends. You'll regret your words tomorrow." I should have remembered . . . I'll try harder from now on.

I've started to call you a dozen times and hung up. I jumped every time my phone rang, hoping it would be you. These two weeks have given me a lot of time to be lonely and a lot of time to think. We've been attacking each other, hurting each other, and getting nowhere but distant. Probably because we never really talk about the things that really bother us, things that we didn't even notice until we started living together most of the time. You thought I was a neatnik because everything used to be perfect when you came to visit. You never saw my closets. I thought you were organized. You are, except for your laundry, and your bills, and getting your books back to the library on time. We've spent a lot of time lately arguing over our trivial differences. I don't think these things are the real problem. The real problem is that we've forgotten to talk about the good things.

I don't tell you any more how much I enjoy rehashing my day and yours every evening. Or how much I appreciate your patience. Especially when I remember five blocks away that I forgot to unplug the coffee pot. I haven't told you how nice it is to look up from my book and watch you playing with my cat. She never took much to anyone before. Maybe she's pleased with the collar you bought.

I miss seeing your clothes in my closet. I miss the smell of your soap and the scent of you on my sheets. Callie sits in front of the door at six o' clock. She's lonely too.

How did this happen? We forgot we were different. We forgot that some of those differ-ences were what made us excited about each other and how trivial the other differences were. We also seem to have forgotten how to "make nice."

I'm writing this because I want it to be for the record. And also because I'm a little scared. It isn't everything I wanted to say. But I'd like the chance to say the rest, to start again—if not with a clean slate at least with my best eraser—to remember always how much you mean in my life, all our good times and feelings, and my best behavior. I also promise to respect your confidences and not to tread on your softer edges. Please forgive me. Please call.

Love,

Linda

P.S. | When you wonder how you both let your relationship disintegrate:

Do think hard about what has happened and why.

Do analyze the ways in which you both can change your conduct to improve the situation. Is it realistic to expect such change?

Do let your partner know that your relationship is important to you and you want it to improve.

Do accept responsibility for your part in what has happened.

Do share with your partner your analysis of the situation and openly invite input. It's a joint problem. It should be a joint solution.

Do communicate openly, freely, fully.

Don't lay guilt trips on your partner. You want this to be constructive. Who needs to be mired in a sorry relationship? You want a better relationship? Make it better. Together.

Let's Try Again

If at first you don't succeed,
try, try again.
—Aphorism

bis feelings

E very relationship runs into trouble at one time or another. Rarely indeed does the course of true love run smoothly. Word leads to word and suddenly it's an argument. Interests diverge, insecurities clash with indifference, expectations are frustrated, and jealousy is never far away. These things are part of every couple's existence and sometimes result in separation.

But if the parties truly valued the relationship, it is possible that the remembrance of how happy they were and the realization of how unhappy they are will induce them to attempt a reconciliation.

It takes a great deal of courage to be the first to say "Let's try again." A successful reunion can make the effort worthwhile. I have written a lot of "let's try again" letters but mailed very few.

I should have mailed more.

---

his Letter

Dearest . . .

I thought of calling. Got as far as picking up the phone and dialing the number. It rang once, but I got scared and hung up. Anyway, it was me.

I wasn't really sure what to say. The breakup came so fast that, even though I've had a lot of time to think about it, I'm not really sure what happened. We've had other arguments before and gotten over them. But not this time. One moment together, the next apart. Nothing. All over.

Yet when I look back on the time we spent together, things seemed so perfect. We were so happy. Remember how people used to see us walk down the street holding hands and would smile at us? Our happiness made them happy. We were always planning things, doing things, had more friends than we could keep up with. I don't understand how so much love could simply evaporate; how two people who were always telling each other how much they cared suddenly stopped caring.

I don't think we have stopped. I know I haven't. I miss you almost every moment, and when I don't miss you it's because I pretend you're with me and I talk to you. That's true. You know, every night when I get into bed I tell you about my whole day—just the way I used to when we'd call each other late at night.

Of course, now you're not there to advise and guide me. And I can't comfort you the way I used to when things went wrong.

And going to sleep isn't as tough as getting up. I used to bounce out of bed, looking forward to each day. I knew that sometime during that day we'd talk or see each other and, no matter what kind of day it had been, it would wind up a great day— a beautiful day. Now it seems to rain all the time. The whole climate of my life has changed.

I keep asking myself when the clouds started to roll in. When did the chill winds begin to blow?

For my part, it must have been when I started taking us for granted. I figured you'd just always be there. I stopped working at "us."

I have paid a severe price for my indifference. Loneliness is a disease and I am sick without you. Nor do I confuse lonely with being alone. There have been so many times since we parted when I have been surrounded by others and still felt lonely because you weren't there.

Losing you was like experiencing a death, and experiences like that change one. Words like "communication" and "commitment," words that once were important to you are now equally important to me.

I want you to know that all the dreams we had I still dream. All the plans we made, I still want to make come true. Those dreams, those plans—they belong to us and to no one else in the entire world. They were part of who we were and who I want us to be once more.

I'd like us to try again, not just to recapture what we had; rather, to build upon it.

I still believe in you. I still believe in us.

In a few days, I am going to try to gather enough courage to call again. This time I'll let the phone ring until you answer it, because this time I know what I'll say when you do:

I still love you.

Sid

ḣer feelıŋgs

What do you do if you drop a cherished vase, a piece of the china your grandmother left you, your favorite coffee mug? You get out your super glue and try to stick it back together. The result may be a functional object with a few rough edges. Or like Humpty-Dumpty, it may resist all your efforts.

A good relationship that has been damaged is not necessarily beyond repair. We learn from our mistakes and hope not to repeat them. If you caused the breakage, tell him what made you so careless with a precious possession. And once you fix it, be sure not to let it come unglued again.

ḣer letter

Dear . . .

Where have you been all my life? I know where you were for part of it. But I really messed it up. How I miss you. I miss your face, your quiet low voice. How I wish I could have another chance to share my life with you.

A year ago, I wasn't ready to share anything. I wanted to keep my freedom. I had been single such a short time that I wasn't willing to be part of a couple yet. You wanted very much to share my life, my activities, my friends, and I kept pushing you away. You kept coming back, but you never criticized or complained. I thought you were too passive. I couldn't understand why you were always so anxious to please me, why you were so nice.

What a dope I was. Only when you weren't there any more did I realize how much I enjoyed your company, that you had been genuinely interested in me, that it was nice to have someone be nice.

Now when I look up from the paper on a Sunday morning, the kitchen seems so empty. If I walk through the park, I expect to see you waiting on the third bench on the left. I've taken many walks there recently. I've even walked near your office about noon, thinking I might bump into you on your way to lunch. I don't know what I would have said.

That's why I'm writing instead. It would have been difficult to say these things face to face. I didn't appreciate you. Before I knew you, I equated love with noise and turmoil, wild fights and wilder reunions. I didn't know that a relationship could mean peaceful companionable silence and pleasant conversation, gentle lovemaking, stability, fulfilled expectation. I didn't know love could be nice.

I want so much for you to give me another chance, but I'll understand if you can't.

Linda

P.S. When you write to say "let's try again":

Do make sure you want to.

Do compare the joy you felt in being together with the sadness you feel in being apart.

Do recall the wonderful times you shared.

Do express sorrow for your part in the breakup and tell what you've learned from the experience.

Don't hesitate to suggest getting together again if that's what you want. The possible rewards are great. At worst, you'll be where you are now (and facing it more realistically).

Don't take all the blame on yourself. It's rarely all one party's fault.

Will You Marry Me?

If our two loves be one, or thou and I
Love so alike, that none do slacken, none can die.
—John Donne, "The Good-Morrow"

ḣıs ꞃeeLıɳꬶs

The idea of a marriage proposal by letter initially may seem a little strange; something reserved for mail-order brides. But in a mobile world, people meet and part and frequently stay in touch by writing to one another. Distance separates and the Post Office unites. He is overseas in the military, or she is on a long-term business assignment in another country. They attend different universities in cities thousands of miles apart. Once they lived near each other; now they don't.

It is, after all, the most important question that can be asked and it has to be asked when the spirit moves you and the time is right. You may be sitting on a hillside, kneeling by a campfire, or leaning over an old wooden desk in a dormitory, writing to someone you love half a world away.

I have never proposed by letter, but it can't be terribly different than doing so in person. In fact, it may have certain advantages. Erasers for one, in case you think of a better way of saying it.

Since I am on the verge of asking her to marry me, I think if I were to put it in a letter it would go something like this.

ḣis Leɔɔer

Dearest . . .

I have written this letter a hundred times in my mind. Tonight I've written and rewritten it a dozen times. I may rewrite it another dozen before I mail it to you. It has got to be absolutely perfect. You see, I only intend to write one such letter in my entire lifetime. This is it.

Actually, I never imagined writing a letter like this. I pictured the scene so differently. We'd have been out on a date, fancier I think than most. Perhaps I'd have taken you to that beautiful restaurant in the Village, "One if by land . . ." I'd order the best wine and have the pianist play our song. Afterward, we'd linger by the fireplace for a brandy. On the way home, I'd buy you one perfect long-stemmed rose. Back in your apartment, I'd sit you down on the sofa, remove my pocket handkerchief and place it on the floor, then kneeling on it, I'd take your hand in mine and say:

From the moment I first saw you, I've loved you. In my entire life, I had never seen anyone as beautiful. But it wasn't until I really got to know you that I realized you were as beautiful on the inside as on the outside. You are every good thing a person can be: caring and compassionate, sensitive and appreciative, intellectually alive but so completely unpretentious, slow to criticize, quick to praise, ready to forgive, and loving—so wonderfully loving.

I am certain that you are the person God had in mind when he created people.

Is it any wonder that I adore you? I cannot believe, truly cannot believe, that in the history of the world any man ever loved a woman as much as I love you! You are so deep within me that no matter how far apart we are, I feel that we are united, that we are one.

And that is just what I want us to be: one—one before man, one before God, until with His help we become another and pray yet another. . . .

Should that come to pass, I will always be there for you as friend, as lover, as life's partner. My entire life will be dedicated to your happiness so that every day of your life you will know that you have made the right decision. You will be, because you are, the center of my world.

I know that you have other dreams as well, plans for accomplishments of your own. I'll be your biggest booster as you realize those independent goals, establish new ones, and accomplish those as well, just as I know you will be there for me as I work to achieve mine.

And how lucky our kids will be! I read somewhere that the best thing a dad can do for his children is to love their mother and the best thing a mother can do for her children is to love their dad. How lucky, indeed.

I am not so naive as to believe life will be without problems, but I do believe that, loving each other as we do, we will overcome whatever lies ahead of us.

This very moment I love you more than at any other moment, and if you'll wait just a moment longer, I'll love you even more.

Then would I take from my pocket this ring I now hold and cannot wait to slip on your finger as soon as I return home, and ask you that which I ask you now:

Will you marry me?

> *Always and forever,*
> *Sid*

P.S. | When you write your proposal of marriage:

Do read the address on the envelope again. This is one letter you don't want to go astray. (Are you sure you want to entrust it to the U.S. Post Office?)

Do make sure the stamp's on tight!

We don't have any "don'ts" to offer about this letter. You wouldn't be writing it if you weren't sure of your feelings.

Yes . . . Yes!

Yes, yes, a thousand times yes, I'd rather die than say no.
—Anonymous

her feelings

ost girls daydream about the day some young Prince Charming will propose. It's part of the package of illusions that start with scribbling your first name together with his last and proceeds right through a fairy tale wedding and a honeymoon on Fantasy Island. It's fun . . . and it's harmless, providing one is able to wake up and smell the coffee when it counts.

Few women expect to receive a marriage proposal in the mail. Yet, once again, it is a mobile world and frequently people who are in love are forced to sustain their relationship by letter if it is to be sustained at all. If the time is right and the moment moves him to propose, a letter is as good a form of communication as any and better than most.

Besides, if you truly love him, does it matter if his proposal is in a letter . . . or sky writing . . . or smoke signals? You know what the answer will be.

ḥer Leꜩꜩer

Dearest . . .

I received your letter, rushed upstairs to my room, closed the door and, sitting on the edge of my bed, slowly, carefully opened the envelope—almost as if I were afraid to spill any of the precious words. I hadn't heard from you in several days and do so look forward to your letters.

As I read this one my eyes glistened and then, with joy and only with joy, I cried openly. I wanted to hold you in my arms, to kiss you, to press you to me, but you are so very far away. Instead, silly as it may seem, I crossed my arms and held your letter close to my heart murmuring over and over again, "Yes—yes—a thousand times yes!"

Yes, I will marry you.

Yes, I will cherish and care for you and love you 'til the day I die.

Yes, I want to be the mother of our children.

Yes, I want to travel through life with you and grow together.

Yes, I want to experience all that life has to offer and to share it with you.

Yes, I want to be by your side and know that you'll be by mine forever.

And someday I want to reach out and smooth your wrinkled brow and look back with you on a life well lived and well loved.

Oh, yes—yes—yes!!

. . .

P.S. | When you write to accept his proposal of marriage:

Mazel tov!! Cent' anni!!

C H A P T E R   3 4

Goodbye for Now

Parting is all we know of heaven,
and all we need of Hell.
                    —Emily Dickinson, "J 1732"

ḣis feeliṅgs

E ach relationship is different. There is no one right way to proceed from initial encounter to permanent commitment. In fact, it is not constructive to have in mind some "ideal" relationship against which to measure your present one. It's somewhat like idealizing sex after reading a romance novel or a better-bed-techniques manual. Frustration and disappointment can be the only result for the "ideal" is but a concept. Life is real; life is earnest.

One relationship may proceed smoothly and without interruption. Another may be marked by fits and starts. Both can wind up happily, however, providing that the couple in the bumpy relationship exercises a measure of caring, patience, and maturity. The destination, after all, is more important than the journey.

I would have bet that one particular couple I know would have lasted forever. You probably know such a couple. When they break up, it shakes our faith in all relationships. But this couple hasn't really ended their relationship; they've simply put it on hold for a while, feeling the need for some space and time to rethink and reevaluate. They have not said goodbye forever, just for now. I'm still betting on them. From such a "time out" I believe they may return to each other refreshed, renewed and recommitted. Time away frequently makes us cherish time together even more. A stronger relationship can result.

But telling someone you genuinely care for that you need a break can be extraordinarily tricky. It requires all of your communicative skills. You do not want to hurt them. Quite the contrary, you want to keep the prospect of reunion very much alive. This may be the most difficult of all love letters to write.

Let me try my hand at it.

---

his Letter

Dearest . . .

I stopped the world today.

"Getting and spending, we lay waste our lives," wrote the Bard. Not today. Today, I neither got nor spent.

Instead, I drove up the Palisades to Bear Mountain, walked through the fields and around Hessian Lake, sat on a nearby bench and thought. Mostly about us.

We've come so far, you and I. Acquaintances, friends, sweethearts and lovers. So far—and in such a relatively short time. Yet in that short time, I feel I've come to know you so well. Perhaps better than I know myself.

I hadn't intended to get so deeply involved with anyone - not just yet. But, then, you weren't "anyone"; you were, and are, the most special someone I'd ever known. I am so glad we met, so grateful for the time we've had together. I don't regret any of it.

The real question is—what next? Where do we go from here? We seem to be caught up in a momentum of our own making and I am concerned that the tide is sweeping us somewhat too quickly in unplanned directions. I know that if we fail to "take the current when it serves" we risk losing "our venture," but I'm not afraid of that. I believe in us. I also believe that each of us is responsible for the course of our own life and that we share responsibility for the course of the life that may someday be ours. We just can't "let things happen" and ignore that responsibility.

Right now I need some time apart. I need to rethink, reevaluate many things in my life including us and our relationship. I know that whatever may have come up between us in the past, you love me enough to give me that time. Neither of us wants to make a mistake. It's important that we both be sure about where we want to go and whether we ought to go there together.

I do not know how much time I will need nor do I believe artificial limits should be set. Let's both agree to go separate ways awhile, free to follow our own paths. But please join with me in a silent prayer that somewhere up ahead those paths will meet so that we can continue our journey together.

Sid

ÞER FEELIŊGS

Sometimes someone comes into your life like a windstorm, a thunderclap. Their being seems so much in tune with your own and the promise of a relationship so heady that you don't look backward or sideways. You plunge right in. No matter what interests unite you and what similarities exist, elements of the other person are so different, so completely opposite from yours that unknown territory, mystery, and adventure beckon. You are fascinated. The sun shines in every corner of your new exciting life.

We met at work, introduced by our mutual friend and boss— a perfectly socially acceptable meeting. He commented on a book on my desk, and our first brief conversation told me he was familiar with many of my favorite authors. We continued our conversation at lunch. . .and at dinner. Greater miracle! He was a poet, too. What's more, he read mine, liked it, understood it. Who could ask for anything more? Within two weeks, I was working with him on his poetry journal, an effort we continued for several years. We worked well together. Ideas and inspiration flowed. His friends were exciting, most of them involved in some way with literature. Many of them were a little zany, some of them wildly so. We spoke of future projects and the hope of leaving the workaday world behind.

Our relationship was great fun—and very stormy. He was big on dramatic partings. His letters were postmarked Dublin, Salt Lake City, Texas, Germany. He pondered joining the Russian Navy or the IRA. He never considered the Foreign Legion as far as I know, but maybe it no longer exists. I was involved with a walking cataclysm, a dervish. It lasted several years. We said goodbye, but we never said goodbye forever. We remained friends and half-friends for many years. I still prize his letters. *One* of his "goodbye for now" letters follows.

LETTER RECEIVED FROM HIM

Dearest . . .

You still are to me. Nonetheless, I must tell you this. I think you may not understand and will possibly find it distressing, but I am leaving the monastery and moving to the Hotel Zanzibar with a woman named Roxie Lutz, who packs herring.

This is not a snap decision!

I have weighed everything and have concluded that there is more serenity contained in Roxie's index finger than in the entire Book of Job. She know's where it's at! And I hope you're satisfied!

I do not wish this to become a "Dear John" letter, so I will stop now. I know you wish us good luck.

We will be married in Upper Jay, New York on the 23rd. I never dreamed I would realize myself in such an uncanny fashion, That's for sure! And I always liked herring.

My tender regards to Laurie. And to Diane.

And Charles.

And to you and good luck.

No gifts please.

> *Love always,*
>
> *M.*

P.S. | When you write your letter to say "goodbye for now":

Do write with affection.

Do word your letter very carefully. You want a little breathing space, not a grand finale.

Do be sure you tell your partner how much the relationship has meant to you until now. If you've had problems, this is not the time to thrash them out. That can wait until you've had time to say hello again.

Don't begin your letter with "If only you had. . ." This is not the time for blame, but for reaffirmation.

Don't specify an arbitrary time period for your separation. The fact that you have decided to separate temporarily should be enough to tell you of your confusion. Allow yourself unfettered freedom to make a very important decision.

Goodbye Forever

To leave is to die a little . . .
We leave behind a bit of ourselves
Wherever we have been.
    — Edmond Haraucourt, "Rondel de l'adieu"

We would often be sorry if our wishes were gratified.
                    —Aesop

his feelings

Most relationships do not end suddenly. Perhaps it would be better if they did. There would be a period of intense hurt and some considerable anger, and it would be over. Instead, once the end comes into view, we go through a process of denial and acceptance—denial and acceptance that leaves the participants twisting in the wind. Sometimes, for sure, Humpty-Dumpty doesn't so much fall as slip and he can be put back on the wall. But once the shell cracks, it's all over. Attempted reconciliation only prolongs the agony. One day you recognize that whatever there was between you is no more.

What makes a relationship special is that those in it feel special. There is a confidence, a trust, secret words and looks, unspoken understandings that insulate the two of you even in a crowd. You feel special because you are special—special to one other person. Then, for whatever reason or for no reason, the feeling is gone. You are naked in the world once again; loneliness replaces love.

There are two choices: to continue CPR to a dead romance or to acknowledge that it's over and to move on with your life. I always favor telling the truth. But I believe in telling it gently,

Letters of farewell require great grace whether you are the one saying goodbye or the one to whom goodbye has been said. The bromide, "what goes round, comes round," is true and, since we tend to stay within fairly well-defined social circles, the chances of encountering a former lover are considerable. But grace provides its own reward even if you never see each other again. Endings are not easy, but they can be accomplished with style and without embarrassment.

We never saw each other again, but the following letters enabled us to do so with equanimity if ever we did.

his Letter

Dearest . . .

This is the most difficult letter I've ever written. Words are my business. This should be easier. It isn't.

How I wish there were a clear-cut reason for everything in life. Wouldn't it be nice if there were a "because" for every "why"? Sometimes things happen, situations change, feelings you once had you no longer have, and there is no special reason—surely no blame.

For some time now I think we have both come to realize that our relationship is not working, not working for either of us. A

relationship should be fun, fulfilling, rewarding. Of course, it's important to work at it, and we have—so very hard. But when it becomes more work than either of us must feel it's worth, when it stops being rewarding, when it gives more pain than pleasure, it's time to end it.

I cannot even say "I'm sorry." Yes, I do regret that the future will not be ours to share. But I do not regret the part of our lives we have shared. The love that was ours will always be ours. My life means more, will always mean more, because you were part of it.

You gave me the happiest moments of that life. I never felt as loved as I did in your arms, never as special. I am such a different, I hope a better person today because of your influence: calmer, more genuinely secure, more comfortable with the world and with myself.

You gave me so much! I ought to be able to make you happy in return. Clearly, I am no longer able to do so. Everything I say, everything I do, seems to be wrong these days. I no longer know how to please you, and the hurt I'm causing you pains me even more.

I have retreated within myself. No wonder you cannot find the fellow you once knew or make him happy any more.

I want so much for you to be happy and I need to feel that happiness, too. If we cannot find it together, it's best if we find it separately. The right guy is out there for you. I wish it were me, but it isn't. Maybe she's out there for me as well. I hope so.

I'll never forget you. I couldn't if I wanted to. You have become part of who I am. But it's time for both of us to leave and to get on with our lives. So . . .

"Go from me. Yet I feel that I shall stand
Henceforward in thy shadow. Nevermore
Alone upon the threshold of my door
Of individual life I shall command
The uses of my soul, nor lift my hand
Serenely in the sunshine as before,

Without the sense of that which I forebore-
Thy touch upon the palm. The widest land
Doom takes to part us, leave thy heart in mine
With pulses that beat double. What I do
And what I dream includes thee, as the wine
Must taste of its own grapes. And when I sue
God for myself, He hears that name of thine
*And sees within my eyes the tears of two."**

Sid

Dear . . .

"Well, I have lost you; and I lost you fairly;
In my own way, and with my full consent.
Say what you will, kings in a tumbrel rarely
Went to their deaths more proud than this one went.
Some nights of apprehension and hot weeping
I will confess; but that's permitted me;
Day dried my eyes; I was not one for keeping
Rubbed in a cage a wing that would be free.
If I had loved you less or played you slyly
I might have held you for a summer more,
But at the cost of words I value highly,
And no such summer as the one before.
Should I outlive this anguish—and men do—
I shall have only good to say of you." †

Thank you for my yesterdays.
Thank you for my tomorrows.

A.

---

*Sonnets from the Portuguese (No. 111), by Elizabeth Barrett Browning (1806–1861).

†Sonnet XLVII of *Fatal Interview*, by Edna St. Vincent Millay. From *Collected Sonnets*. Revised and Expanded Edition. Harper & Row, 1988. Copyright © 1931, 1958 by Edna St. Vincent Millay and Norma Millay Ellis. Reprinted by permission of Elizabèth Barnett, Literary Executor.

ber FeeLings

Did you ever ride the cyclone at Coney Island? Your teeth shake in your head, your heart clutches in your chest, your bones feel like they are separating from your body. When you are poised on the crest of the highest loop, you feel like your mind is separating as well. Who would pass up a thrill like that?

Sane people. They might even opt for a merry-go-round. Listening to pleasant music, experiencing a gentle rise and fall, covering the same familiar ground again and again—and knowing they won't go off the track or over the edge.

Once I couldn't get enough of roller-coasters. Craziness has a certain appeal. It promises freedom, letting go of responsibility, sheer fun without regard for consequences, a constant state of tension and expectancy. When the roller-coaster is your relationship, all these facets come into play. The slow ratcheting climb to the heights, the precipitous plunge, then climb, fall, and climb, fall again.

Such a relationship is almost awe-inspiring, but it can't last. It's too exhausting. Even if you hold the world's record for riding roller-coasters, the time comes when you begin to think of merry-go-rounds, or maybe even the rest of the amusement park out there.

ber Letter

Dear . . .

Hey, honey. Flash on this. Enough is enough. No more pulling you out of gas-filled rooms or body-filled bars. I've had it. Your last letter was the last straw. I have no desire to join you. Actually, I have the desire but not the stamina. I've never said no before and meant it. This time I do.

My job here is a good one and I'm not giving it up for some new wild ride around the country or the world. We'd be back and broke and living in some dump on C_____ Street again. And I'd be out of a job.

No thanks.

No, it wasn't the letter about Roxie. The line about getting married was the giveaway. Now if you had said you and she were opening a herring factory, I might have believed you. But I do wish you good luck.

How will I get you out of my head? I probably never will. I never had so much fun and so much trouble in my life at the same time. And I know I'll never get you out of my heart. You're entrenched. But you will have to live there as friend only from now on. Say hello to Anwar. Be well, my Coney Island comet.

Love always,
Linda

P.S. | When you write your letter of final farewell:

Do make it a fare*well* letter. You're saying goodbye, but implicit in that word is that you wish your partner well, not ill.

Don't be cruel. Don't write anything ugly. You're not writing a poison-pen letter. Remember, your words can come back to haunt you.

Don't offer false hope that you will begin anew, even if your relationship has been the best of all possible relationships. That is the cruelest cut of all.

C H A P T E R 3 6

A Love Letter to Someone
Much Older

Love, all alike, no season knows, nor clime,
Nor hours, day, month, which are the rage of time.
  —John Donne, "The Sun Rising"

. . . in ages of imagination . . . firm persuasion . . .
removed mountains . . .
  —William Blake, "A Memorable Fancy"

his feelings

She has more than a few years on me but you could never tell it by her energy, her vitality, or her outlook. She is a ball of fire whether in the courtroom or on the dance floor. Over the years we have traveled much of the world together as great, good friends. What an intelligent, stylish, sophisticated, and elegant companion! She has added so much seasoning to the stew of my life.

I've come to depend on her advice—especially in times of personal crisis. She takes a longer view than I do and is both wise and practical. Such a steadying influence. And more than once her good counsel has gotten me out of some relationship problem. A blessed day when I first met her. If she's what an older woman is like, most men don't know what they've been missing!

We haven't seen each other for a while. We sort of keep in touch through Norman who tends bar over at the Jockey Club, a favorite haunt. What a curious way to communicate with such a dear friend. Actually, we'll see each other at a convention in San Diego next month. If I don't write her soon, she'll have my head on a silver platter.

Worse yet, she'll stop teaching me.

ᚺIS LETTER

Dear . . .

    It's been too long!

    Too long since we cleared a dance floor . . . strolled a beach . . . opened a bottle of champagne . . . talked quietly. I miss your friendship, your warmth, your sage advice. I seem to be surrounded by the crème de la crème of shallow. I miss your depth. I miss you.

    There is so much to be said for experience. I learn the moment we meet and keep learning until the moment we part. I know younger, my dear friend, but I sure as hell don't know better!

    I can't wait to see you next month. You'll be the finest-looking woman there and I'll be heartbroken if you aren't my companion for every social event they've scheduled. But mostly, let's make time to talk. Your "Mr. Wonderful" has an active social life but hasn't been able to find just that one right person. Am I searching too hard? Am I looking in the wrong places? You see, I give my advice to others and you give yours to me. Guess I still need you in my life. Guess I always will.

    Norman sends his love. The first toast is always for you.

    See ya!

                Sid

ḣer feelings

If we're lucky, we have many loves in our lives—of many kinds. Love is no respecter of age, that's sure. We can cite long loves and marriages that have surmounted the seemingly impossible barrier of a great span of years. We also know of love that endures as lifelong friendship and never encompasses physical love. Such a love might be the grandparent who first understood your childish fear of the dark and helped you, with a flashlight, flush out the monsters lurking in closets and behind trees. It might be the teacher who first opened a magic door of learning. The uncle who taught you the foxtrot. The aunt who took you to hear your first symphony. The colleague at work who first eased you into the office routine and helped you repeatedly in your career. May we all have at least one golden oldie in our memory. Mine is Henry.

The time to tell someone of your love is always now. And it's even more important if that someone is older. What if you missed the opportunity to tell them what they have meant to your life? I hope I didn't wait too long to write the following.

ḣer letter

Dear Henry,

I haven't seen you in so long. We haven't talked. Life gets so busy and we neglect important things. I hope you are well and happy. My life has taken at least half the twists and turns we used to talk about each morning or during lunch at my desk. None of them are as interesting yet as yours have been. But I still take my "Ten-Minute Tour" at least once a week, and I think of you each time I do. Sometimes it's an actual walk in the garden to see what flower has opened its face to the light, or to watch the expressions

223

on people's faces as I perform some errand, to imagine the lives behind the eyes, as you taught me. Sometimes I take my tour by resting my head on the desk and imaging myself into my "pleasant place," the open beach where we sometimes walked. The sun warms my shoulders and the breeze lifts my hair. I can smell the sea. What a wonderful gift you gave me.

I miss you. My job at C____ was interesting. So many people with fascinating stories of life in a different world. Some of their stories were of horror that should never occur again. But they survived it all and relished life. As you did. You are the greatest relisher I've ever known. You took me on ten-minute tours of La Scala, old Vienna, 1920s tenements and speakeasies on the Lower East Side.

With you, I heard the first shots at Saravejo and the cries and shouts of freedom and peace. I learned of the terrors of typhoid and the enormous courage of immigrants. I learned fragments of other languages and other cultures. And I learned love. Your courtly manner and attention revived me during a very difficult time in my life. You were also experiencing terrible trial, the loss of your lifelong companion and love. Much later in our friendship, we talked lightly about the love we might have shared if forty years and a continent had not separated us so long. What "mowing" we might have made. But I want you to know that all the talk wasn't all light. You have enriched my life and I will always have a special love for you. May you live and be well.

Always,
Linda

P.S. When you write your letter to your
older friend:

Do remind them of the many ways in which they have
touched your life and the permanence of your loving
thoughts of them. All of us want to live in the memories of our friends and lovers.

Do stay aware of your friends' whereabouts. It's so
easy to lose track of people we seldom have the
opportunity to see.

Don't procrastinate. If your friend is much older than
you are, you may miss the opportunity to tell them of
your feelings.

C H A P T E R   3 7

A Love Letter to Someone
Much Younger

Age cannot wither, nor custom stale . . . infinite variety.
—Shakespeare, *Antony and Cleopatra*

his feelings

She is about to celebrate her thirty-second birthday. I have just celebrated my fifty-second. When she was born I was a junior in college. By the time she entered high school, I was already a father with two children ages eight and six. The numbers just don't add up. Nevertheless, I truly love her.

No, I am not trying to relive my youth. This is a wonderful time of life with plenty of its own rewards. Nor can it fairly be said that the age difference assures me some kind of control in the relationship. It's a remarkably equal one.

Although some of our references are different (I compared

Tyne Daly's performance in Gypsy to Ethel Merman's but it was a meaningless comparison to one who never heard Merman), they are minor and terribly insignificant. Our interests are overwhelmingly the same. She is exceedingly bright, the most intuitive and analytic person I know, and is imbued with a full measure of grace and sophistication.

Ours is a symbiotic relationship. She has refreshed my outlook, renewed my enthusiasm, helped me discuss my feelings more openly, and taught me that it wasn't always necessary to push so hard. I've provided a steadiness, a longer view of problems that arise, an optimism that things generally work out for the best, a patient friend who listens carefully and, I hope, advises well.

We do not feel the age difference when we are together yet it is always there. It is a limiting factor on how free we feel to carry what we have further. She is entitled to build her life with some one who will experience its joys with the newness that only the first time around can provide. She is also entitled to be free from the concern of empty later years if I am gone. Are there counter arguments to these concerns? Of course there are. Is each couple a distinct entity which must be considered separately and do some May–December relationships work wonderfully? The questions answer themselves. It's only important that we know our own feelings.

We see each other every so often. We talk on the telephone all the time. And a great many of the letters in this book were either first written to her or were written with her in mind.

I suppose it is possible that in time our view of the significance of the age difference will change. Anything's possible. But, oh, if 1938 had only been 1948!

his LeTTeR

Dearest . . .

I love Nyack! Sitting on the terrace watching the sailboats bob up and down, looking at the cars scurrying across the bridge in the distance, enjoying the proliferation of flowers draped over my railing. It's just a lovely summer's evening.

Remember how many people I had on this terrace last week? I feared it would come crashing down into the Hudson. But it was a grand party and I surmise it is becoming an annual event. Thanks again for helping me clean up afterward.

Know what I enjoyed most? Not the food (I have leftovers to feed a militia), nor Teddy at the piano, not even having the kids home. It was you, when everyone else had gone, sitting here discussing your problem with me. It makes me feel so good that when you have a concern you come to me for advice. It enables me to give you something that perhaps some others—some younger others—can't: the benefit of experience. Besides, when you come to me it's sort of a vote of confidence, of trust, and I relish it.

We certainly seem to have proved ourselves a good team—my counsel and your creative implementation. Problem ended, resolution assured. I'll tell you this, you are one quick study!

We're a good team in other ways, too. You enliven my life with your enthusiasm, leaven my life with your absence of pretension, enrich my life with your insights. I just seem to enjoy it all so much more when we are together.

And, perhaps, I add something to your life as well. I'd like to think so. At least you've succeeded in making me feel so. If there are a certain numbers of years I cannot give you, will never be able to give you, at least I can share with you the benefit of my having lived them, the knowledge if not the wisdom they have given me, and a certain degree of comfort.

There is much to be said for youth. You'll get no argument in this quarter on that. But there is also, I suppose, some value in having lost the hard edge, the aggressiveness, the impatience and temper. I have been in the barrel long enough to mellow a bit and may, after all, be worth sipping.

Someday, of course, you will meet just the right young man. I only hope that he cherishes you as I do and will be as good to you as I am. Or, at least that he genuinely tries. Sometimes that's enough, too. On that day, I will become an anecdote.

And on occasion you will remember that once upon a time someone gave you all his love and asked nothing in return but your happiness.

Sid

hER FEELINGS

When we see a man with a younger woman, we seldom question whether she is his companion or his daughter. If indeed she is his companion, we accord him status and admiration. He is viewed as powerful, one who knows what he wants and gets it, and, moreover, one who deserves it. The woman, on the other hand, may be stigmatized as helplessly dependent at best, a gold-digger or tramp at worst.

In the May–December romances with which we are most familiar, the man was the elder partner. A few recent examples are Pablo Casals, Charlie Chaplin, Pablo Picasso, William O. Douglas, Jacob Javits, Groucho Marx. Their public lives and/or fame drew attention to the discrepancy between their ages and those of their partners, but if eyebrows were raised, they didn't remain so for long. The alliances between older women and younger men have received less attention, regardless of the respective stature of the partners. Benjamin Disraeli and William Shakespeare were married to "older women." Jennie Churchill, George Sand (Aurore Dupin), Dorothy Parker, Agatha Christie, and Lucille Ball are a few of the many women who either married or were aligned with younger partners.

Today, the number of women involved in relationships in which they are the elder partners is increasing steadily. Many explanations are plausible: women have better educations, their own financial resources, independence, and freedom to choose, all things once considered mainly the province of males. That doesn't mean that their relationships with younger men don't raise eyebrows, don't cause tongues to wag. With the role switch, the woman often is still viewed as a culprit. The remarks directed against her may not be worse than those faced by older men in a similar position: she is "a fool," "in her dotage," "a cradle-snatcher." Still, the remarks can range from disbelief to outrage and imply that she, more than a man, somehow goes against nature in choosing a younger partner.

The truth is that often she is the chosen. None of us have neon signs on our foreheads indicating our age or status. Most women no longer look their chronological age. They remain attractive long past the years that once marked them "old." Let's be real. Vitality, active interests, intelligence, and experience combined with good physical appearance are a winning combination for anyone in any situation. When we are attracted to another, we transcend many differences and emphasize our similarities to promote a good union. Couples who face a significant age barrier have additional initial and potential ongoing problems. If they weren't already unusual, however, they wouldn't be in a relationship. What about having children, their own or adopted? What about their markedly different stages of life and development? What will happen in ten years, fifteen? Will she become ill, an invalid, while he is still youthful? Will he leave her for someone closer to his own age?

The answer is another question: Who knows? No relationship, no marriage, comes with a guarantee despite our vows and intent. And the lack of a guarantee is not predicated on age. Each of us has only one big expiration date. Our shelf life is as long as we choose to make it.

ḥer Lecter

Dear . . .

They just don't know what to make of us, do they? I didn't either for a while. Now I think we're doing just fine, and there's no reason why we shouldn't continue to do so.

Funny . . . I was on the opposite end of the seesaw once—a long relationship and good in part. It produced three children, good people and all fine, thanks. And it didn't stop because of the age difference but because of the oldest and truest explanation: irreconcilable differences. We didn't grow apace; we grew apart. Maybe if we talked to each other, learned more about each other, before we married, we might have realized how very different we were in every way. But we had been dance partners for four years, and we skated well together. We figured that was good enough. How far wrong could we go?

Well, it wasn't all dancing. Once we had children and had to sit out the numbers, the division between us was greater. It became a chasm we couldn't cross. I'm not sorry. I like the results of that union and I wouldn't change them.

What does this say about our future? Nothing. We can't predict anything or predicate our future on past relationships. We fumbled our way into this. I resisted it. I thought you were starry-eyed, unwilling to see reality.

Well, you taught me. I was the arbitrary bigot. I could have forsworn you and never had the opportunity to spend these years with you. I would have denied myself your love and a relationship with a partner more suited to me, more like me, than any other I have known.

I guess it's lucky that I have no money or power. No one questions your motives, just your sanity. At least they questioned it in the beginning. No one seems to notice us much anymore. If they do, it doesn't bother me. I'm having too much fun. I don't think of you as a "younger man." You are my love.

Will it last? Who knows? We've discussed all the issues. Some weren't part of our consideration even before we met. Others aren't in our foreseeable future. But for a while they were all we ever talked about. What a bore. Now we talk about what we like, enjoy, and do together. That's a lot more fun.

Everyone in a relationship is working against the odds. At least that's what the statistics show. Maybe our odds are better because we worked out a lot of worries and fears before we started. I'm willing to place my bet on us.

Love,

Linda

P.S. | When you write your letter to your younger friend or lover:

Do have fun. Remember: you are special. Love is no respecter of age or anything else.

Do stress the qualities that brought you together and that continue to strengthen the bonds between you.

Do let your partner know how much you care, how much you value your relationship. In this respect, you're just like any other couple.

233

Don't minimize the differences your different ages make. He or she is as much aware of them as you are. Hiding or masking your misgivings won't make them go away. Trying to deny your own age will make you look like a fool.

Don't pay any attention to what "other people" say. You'll probably outlast their criticisms or comments (which they have no business offering).

A "Love Letter" to a Parent

Lord, have mercy on them both
as they took care of me when I was little.
—The Koran

"Reverence for parents" stands written among
the three laws of most revered righteousness.
—Aeschylus, *The Suppliants*

his feelings

When I called my own mother, Ethel Bernstein, in Anaheim to tell her I was including a letter to her in this book, she was pleased but surprised. I thought about that for some time after the conversation ended. Why should she be surprised?

Therein lies the lesson. With what devotion our parents raised us! Through sickness and injury, worrying about our education and our welfare, frequently not knowing how the bills would get paid, their devotion was constant. There was love in their smile, in the food they fed us, in the way the house was kept, in each wrinkle and in every gesture. Were our parents always right? Of course not! But they were always our parents. Did they always do the best thing? Surely not, but they always did the best they knew how to do.

Let me tell you a story. When Michael was born and Joyce and I brought him home from the hospital, I stood by the side of his crib and trembled. Suddenly I was aware of all that lay ahead of me to help raise him properly. Would I be equal to the task? With awe and wonder I realized as never before the debt I owed my mother who, widowed young, raised three children alone, without benefit of formal education and without an extra dollar in her purse. Faced with parenthood for the first time, for the first time I appreciated parenthood.

Not every parent is a good parent and I'm not naive enough to believe so. But as Rabbi Kirshblum taught me, the Commandment says "Honor thy Father and thy Mother." It doesn't mention any exceptions and it doesn't mention any conditions.

So tell me, if I've written love letters to Lynn and to Myra, to Joyce and to Andra, shouldn't I also write one to Ethel?

his Letter

Dear . . .

It's been too long since I've written and I apologize. I know we speak on the phone but because of the distance we keep the conversations short —and anyway it's not the same.

Family news first. Michael is seeing someone, seriously I think. I'm overjoyed, especially since I introduced them. She's an absolutely lovely young woman, a psychologist–career counselor, bright, dedicated, energetic and upbeat. If it's to be, may fortune smile on them!

Mother, grandmother and, who knows, maybe in a while a

great-grandmother. Wouldn't that be something! I'm not exactly sure what the definition of a "matriarch" is but I bet that once you're a great-grandmother they have to let you into the club.

You know my children really are yours as well since so many of the lessons you taught me were passed on intact to them. Even the things you used to do when I was young, I did when they were young. I talked to them all the time—never down and never baby-talk. They were always being read to and were surrounded by books and music and art. God was a constant presence in our home as were the ideas of sharing, caring and concern—" social responsibility" I think they call it these days. Fancy-shmancy. And the stories you told to help me overcome problems that arose. I told them to my kids over and over again.

Remember the one about the seamstress who was worried because she made a knot while darning the King's socks. He thought it was the strongest stitch he'd ever seen and made her his Queen. A great tale when a child fears the consequences of making mistakes! You seemed to have just the right story for each occasion. Thought I'd forgotten, huh?

No, Mom, I've not forgotten a thing—not a thing. I've not forgotten the nights you sat by my bed when I had an earache nor the help you gave me each week when I tried to learn my spelling words. I've not forgotten the hours you spent reading to me nor teaching me to cook even though I was "a boy." (Did that ever come in handy—both in school and while raising the kids!) I've not forgotten seeing you light the sabbath candles that brought God into our home each week nor the stories of your own youth that gave life continuity. I've never forgotten your holding the family together after Pop died and going back to work in the factory after almost 20 years away.

You taught me the value of giving 150% of myself 100% of the time—another five-dollar term, "work ethic." You taught me that there is never a compromise with truth—it's either so or it "ain't."

Most of all, you taught me that we are each responsible for our own lives. What we make of it is up to us. "Quit your complaining!" Remember?

You know, of course, that I'm writing this book on love letters. I'm including this one to you. You were my first girl. You're still my best. I do love you, Mom. I don't think I had to put it in writing for you to know—but, heck, why not? "Assume nothing, my child, assume nothing."

I'll call you Friday night. Do get some rest. You've earned it.
Sid

ber feelings

Mother. Father. The two words that conjure up our vision of a first and "perfect" love for us: a love based on *our* interests, on our growth as individuals—a love all-enveloping, all-enduring, all-forgiving. For most of us these two words or their variations carry us in mind and heart back home, a place of security and warmth, of refuge, the place, according to Robert Frost, where if you go, "they have to take you in." And where they will, gladly.

Bandagers of scraped knees, banishers of night terrors, the cheering section at baseball games and ballet recitals, Brownie and Cub Scout leaders, homework helpers, caretakers and confidantes, problem-solvers or willing listeners. They adapted their roles and attitudes as they guided you from helpless dependence through awkward adolescence to independence, granting you new freedoms at each stage, respecting your individuality, and fostering the growth of the person you now are.

In short: ideal parents—what most of us didn't have and won't be. And almost all parents fall short of this ideal. When we are children, we are acutely aware of our parents' failings, minor or major. Other children's parents are *perfect*. Not ours. Ours are short-sighted, demanding, dictatorial, critical, narrow-minded. As we ourselves age and acknowledge our own shortcomings, we are increasingly aware of their fortitude, their perseverance, their long experience, their wisdom, the accuracy of their knowledge of the world and its workings. If they have failed us in some measure, we can accept that they are human, with imperfections, just like us.

Some cultures revere the elderly, according them respect and honor, seeking their counsel. America is a nation that reveres youth instead, that institutionalizes one day a year for mothers, one for fathers. If we live at great distances from our parents, we send off a small gift, a hasty note or card, follow it up with a phone call. If we are near, we take them out for brunch or dinner. Another year. Our duty done. After all, Mom and Dad understand how busy we are.

The old adage that a parent can take care of nine children but that nine children can't care for one parent holds more than a grain of truth. As many of our parents now survive to a greater age, we find our roles reversed. We become the caretakers, or at least the co-dependents. The switch can be surprising, discomfiting, even burdensome. Nevertheless, no matter what the burden or how long it lasts, we are staggered by the extent of our grief when we finally lose our parents, the embodiment of ultimate love, our lifeline to our past.

Don't reserve a special day to tell your parents of your love. Mother's Day and Father's Day are nice for flowers and barbecues, but any day is the right day to write your parents a love letter. Just be sure you don't wait until it's too late.

her Letter

Dear Mother,

We haven't always found it easy to talk to each other. I was a silent child, not confiding. You say you were baffled by my silence, my difference from my sisters. Not until I had my own children did I begin to understand you.

How hard it must have been for you when I came along. You were so ill. Times were so hard. There you were in Coral Gables, in a place you hated, a hinterland then. Each morning, you found the front porch draped with snakes our dog had killed: water moccasins and rattlers. You were glad when we packed up and moved back to Indiana. We didn't stay long. By the time I was three, we had moved twice again. What was it like for you to move so often, to be far from your relatives, to have to make new friends with every new year, to have each child born in a different city?

I don't remember the first moves. My first memory of the third house is a dirt-walled cellar with a ledge where you kept your jellies and preserves, dark red and purple jewels gleaming in half light. In our house in Philadelphia, I remember trailing you up the attic stairs, watching you open the blue and white enamel pan and sprinkle brandy and wine on the fruit cakes you made each year. I always have some around for the holidays. I don't like the cake, just the fragrance. A remembrance, a token.

Most of my early memories of you are of fragrance: a waft of orange from yeast rolls rising in loaf pans atop the radiators; the rich scent of chocolate brownies or warm bread fresh from the oven on a winter afternoon; a drift of lilac or the faint woods odor of violets, your favorite flowers; tomatoes and spice simmering in an enormous pot; sharp citrus tang—key lime pie.

What a dope I was! I used to envy the kids who had store-bought cookies, mallomars and oreos. I know better now. I never eat dessert unless I make it—the way you taught me.

I also envied those kids their store-bought clothes. It wasn't until you taught me to put in a sleeve without a pucker, to turn a collar, to finish a seam that I really appreciated my embroidered or smocked blouses, my fitted suits, my capes and cloaks, my dress with the seventy buttons.

How many times you stitched me into a dress as I went out the door. "They'll never notice it on a galloping horse," was your comment if a hasty stitch wasn't perfect. But you noticed, and fixed it before I wore the dress again. Each stitch had to be perfect, "for the gods see everywhere."

Mom, you'd be appalled at what you'd find in the stores and on the racks today—not just at the high prices, but at the cheap fabrics, the seams that fall apart at the first washing, the stitches you can catch your nose in, the plastic buttons that fall off after one wearing.

You're still the artist. And I'm a good apprentice, thanks to you. You instructed me in pursuits that have given me pleasures all these years.

You have given me much more through the years: a love of literature, a knowledge of history and mythology, a sense of connection. And you have shown me what loyalty, devotion, and "keeping on keeping on" really mean.

I love you, and I want you to know how much.

Linda

P.S. | When you write your letter to your parent:

Do spend some time recalling the happy events of your childhood. Things that are very significant to you may not be things they remember at all. Telling your parent of these special memories of their demonstrations of love for you is the best gift of love you can return.

Don't bring up unhappy memories or attempt to resolve long-standing difficulties between you. You can write another letter for that purpose at another time.

Don't expect one love letter to resolve difficulties if they do exist. You are reaching out with love and the gesture may help heal any breaches between you, but resolution of problems takes time and commitment, just like love.

Don't wait. Your parents are irreplaceable. You don't want to miss your chance to write this letter.

A "Love Letter" to a Child

*Know you what it is to be a child? . . . it is to believe in love,
to believe in loveliness, to believe in belief; it is to be so
little that the elves can reach to whisper in your ear . . .*
—Shelley, in *The Dublin Review*

his feelings

All relationships evolve but none so much as that between a parent and a child. After all, one party to that relationship changes dramatically over its course. A simple note affixed to a child's pillow saying how proud you are of a particular achievement, the letter to a child away at summer camp or at university, the letter to an adult child in crisis—each is written to the same person, and each is written to a completely different person. All are love letters.

I have been blessed with two wonderful children to whom I have written all their lives. They have written to me, too. Most of the correspondence has been saved. It constitutes the record of our lives, growing up together. The tone of the letters has changed only to the degree that as they got older vocabulary and, I suppose, the level of sophistication changed. But as I review the letters it is clear that I never "wrote down" to them and the love was always constant. Perhaps that is one reason the kids and I are so close.

Following are some letters I've written them over the years: at camp, at the time of their confirmation, as adults.

ḣis Letters

Dear . . .

Welcome to Camp Echo Lake! These are surely the most exciting days of camp: meeting new friends, trying all of the activities, learning the camp customs and traditions. Everything is so new and probably seems strange. But very quickly the newness wears away and before you know it you are in comfortable and familiar surroundings. In fact, I would not be surprised to learn that within a matter of days you feel as if you had been going to camp for years.

I have so many questions to ask you: How was the bus ride up to camp? How is the camp food (do they make leftovers as good as Mommy—mmm, leftovers!)? Have you played ball yet and at what positions? Are you learning to swim?

I am so pleased that the whole family went to visit the camp earlier this year. For now in my mind, I have a picture of the camp and can imagine you at the waterfront or on the baseball diamond or in the arts and crafts bunk.

What are your counselors' names? Do you know where they go to school? And the other boys in the bunk—I am sure that they are all very friendly and anxious to have a good summer. I'll tell you a secret I have found to be true: in order to have a good friend, you must be a good friend. It really is as simple as that.

Sometimes I will write you letters and sometimes I will send you surprises. A surprise will be on its way tomorrow. Not a big surprise, but a nice one anyway.

Until then, have a GREAT summer. I know you will. And eat plenty. If you figure that you are in camp for 56 days, that you will eat 3 meals a day, and that camp costs $1,300, I am paying $7.73 for each meal. So go ahead, have an extra roll. I'm a sport!

With all my love to the best son any dad ever had,
Daddy

The letter that follows my son never read. Thank Heaven! I wrote it some years before his 13th birthday and put it in the vault with instructions that it be given to him the night before his Bar Mitzvah in case I had passed on by then. Both my grandfather and my father had died young and I wasn't taking any chances.

Dear Son,
Tomorrow will be the most important day in your life for tomorrow you will become Bar Mitzvah—a son of the Commandments. I'm sure there will be a big party and all your relatives and friends will be there. It will be festive and it will be fun. A great day!

But before it all begins, I wanted to take a couple of quiet moments alone with you to say some things:

Starting tomorrow you take your place as an adult in the congregation—not only the congregation of our synagogue but, in a larger sense, the congregation of all the people of Israel. That, my son, is not just an honor it is a responsibility. A large responsibility.

It means that your whole life must bear witness to the oneness of God and must be guided by the laws found in the Torah. It also means that you must take the truths found there into the commu-

nity and, in partnership with God, perfect the work of His creation. Because if you don't do it, my son, who will?

You know, the first High Holy Day after you were born, I waited until the sanctuary was empty and then carried you in my arms up to the Ark. I let you touch the soft velvet curtain that hung there and told you that God was all around us. As I kissed your forehead, I prayed that as you grew you would be a source of pride to your parents, to your people, and to Him. And as I watched you grow, I knew that prayer was being answered.

If God had come to me just before you were born (and I'm not altogether certain He didn't) and asked me to describe the son I wanted, I would have described just the sort of boy you were, young man you are, adult you give every evidence of becoming.

Unless I miss my guess, you are probably feeling sad that I won't be there tomorrow. But, I will be there. I'll be sitting upstairs in the balcony—right there with Grandpa Meyer and all the other relatives who now live with God. And, oh, how terribly proud we'll all be!

Not be there? I'll always be there—every step of the way, watching from on high, taking joy in your achievements, asking God to protect you. And whenever you have a question or a doubt, whenever you need my advice or guidance, just go deep inside your conscience and your heart. I'll always be there for you. That's how it is with fathers and sons.

And as to this matter of a gift, I've asked Mom to give you my prayer shawl. She's been saving it for you. Perhaps you'll wear it tomorrow when the Rabbi calls you up, "Michael, the son of Sidney."

I have another gift for you as well. I give you the heritage of your people. Honor it. Add to it.

Mazel tov!

Dad

The next letter I mailed yesterday to my adult daughter:

Dear . . .

Congratulations! How happy I was to learn that you landed the job you so wanted. It seems to me that ability and perseverance paid off.

In that regard, you are the same as you were when you were younger. You've always set your mind on something you wanted and gone straight after it. That's a real strength but the greater strength is that you've never let temporary setbacks get you down. You've always seemed to understand that clouds, no matter how ominous, ultimately blow away. In that, you have been an inspiration to me. Sometimes, the child teaches the parent.

How lucky your new students will be! Their teacher is the happiest, best balanced person I've ever known. In fact, the other day I looked up the word "enthusiasm" in a dictionary and, lo and behold, it had your name and address.

Address. . . that reminds me. I gather you'll be moving. Can I help out—either with two arms that are still fairly strong or a few dollars so you can get some arms that are stronger?

When you get back from your vacation, let's get together. I've always said I'd rather spend my spare time with you than anyone else I know.

You invented fun.

> *Loves ya!*
> *Dad*

ḃER FEELIⴖGS

Letters *from* our children are some of the most important love letters we ever receive—even the first backward, upside-down squiggles and the peculiar facsimile of a being that almost every child first draws: a circle with two tiny dots for eyes, a smile mouth, and two curlicues for arms proceeding from the region of the ears and two others for legs proceeding from the neck region. The letters may be brief or elaborate, they may enclose a cherished object—a "3-D" gift, they may be sad, angry, or demanding. No matter what the content, all the letters I have received from children I construe as love letters. It is hard to choose a favorite. Each has been an unparalleled treasure. One particular letter, from seven-year-old Ryan, seems to me to express love in an ageless dimension. He gave his best, which may be the essence of love in all of us.

ÞER LETTERS

Dear . . .
   Here is the picture of the lion you wanted just like the one Mommy has. I like drawing and painting with you. This lion is in the block style. I mean all the parts of his body are in different color blocks. His mane does not look like it is connected, That is o.k. It is the illusion. I hope you like the lion.
   I used all my best colors for you.
                     Love, Ryan

A letter from one of my sons at age 7 doesn't need much explanation, but I choose to believe he meant "Dad."

Dear Mom,
   I hope you are very happy. You did not let me go see Nightmare on Elm Street. All my friends got to go. They called me sissy, I didn't like the movie we saw insted. And I wish you were dad.
                     Love and kisses, your son.

When I was attending college at night, I found this note from my 8-year-old daughter taped to the kitchen table when I returned home.

Dear Mom,
I don't feel so good. Did you know that?
I have a headack.
*   hedick.*
*   headake.*
Please wake me up when you come home so you can kiss it.
                    Love,
            Your bes sic frend
                    Laurie

Another note on another night read:

Dear Mom,
*   Did your windows ever look emty at night so you wanted your mother to sing to you some more? Here are three (Hershey's) kisses.*

                Love, Laurie

My other son, at age 5, found an undeniable treasure in a parking lot at the back of a store: a big box of bubblegum/baseball card packs. They were new and still in their wrappers. One problem: He was not allowed to chew gum. He unwrapped each package and stored the cherished baseball cards under his bed, where I later found them. He explained his find and promised he would leave things where he found them in the future. "I didn't chew any gum, though," he assured me. His love letter the next day (including a bedraggled piece of gum) read: *"I put all the gom in the gabage. I saved us each 1 pece."*

Laurie, Charlie, and Tony are all grown up now. I miss those letters. I rely on Ryan, Drew, and Tyler for my main correspondence these days.

Dear Ryan, Drew, and Tyler too, even if he can't read this yet,

Isn't kite flying fun? The last time I flew a kite I was seven years old. It was in Philadelphia where I lived when I was a little girl. My kite always went up very high. The wind in March was pretty cold (not like California), but it was just right for kite flying. Our kites weren't bright pieces of cloth like yours. They cost a quarter. You unrolled the piece of diamond-shaped paper and glued it to two sticks. Then you rewound a ball of string very carefully around a stick so that it wouldn't tangle. We had a lot of sugar maple trees around us, every one of them a kite-eating tree, just like Charlie Brown's. Those trees were good for climbing, too. In March, the sap would begin to rise in the trees, while it was still very cold. The icicles on the tree branches were golden brown, not white, because of the maple sap. We ate them like ice pops. I'd like to try it again.

I have new cocoons on the milkweed. Do you remember two years ago when we watched the Monarch butterflies work their way out? How they hung on the cherry tree like orange flowers until their wings dried? I hope you are here in time to see them. Last year, I know I saw Suzie and Snoozy, the last ones we let go.

We'll go to the Big Apple circus when you come. You can get very close to the animals. We'll have cotton candy and hear the calliope play. Circus music always sounds happy. Did you know that's where Callie got her name? She's a happy cat, and when she hangs herself over the couch she looks like one of the big cats in the circus, a gray panther on a tree branch.

I bought some new dyes and a new kind of paper. After you make the paper very wet, you tilt it and pour the dye on. We'll make beautiful skies and beaches. Then peanut butter cookies. We'll show Tyler how to press them down with a fork.

Yesterday I saw a possum in the mimosa tree. Maybe it's one of Ol' Possum's babies. I haven't seen Rocky Raccoon yet. Maybe he found a good cornfield.

I framed your pictures with all your "best colors." If you have any more, please send them quick! And a big kiss and a hug. Or lots of them.

I love you,
Linda

P.S. | When you write your love letters to children:

Do let them know frequently how much they offer you when they let you join in their fun, how much you appreciate their offerings of love, whether those offerings are a word, a letter, a drawing, or their sheer existence.

Do share something with them. You can offer a "gift" to a child of any age, and it needn't be expensive. Bright stamps that come in your "junk" mail, a funny sketch to illustrate your letter, a funny story or a picture from a magazine, a strange leaf. (One favorite was a sea grape leaf with the texture of leather—a great surface to write a letter on.)

Do write to the children in your life *throughout* your life if you want love and understanding to grow between you. Love thrives on awareness of your continuously changing roles.

Don't ask what they did in school today. Ask what they've been thinking about. You may be surprised at the answers you get. Never talk "down." You're bigger, but not necessarily better at communicating.

Don't ever make a promise to a child unless you're pretty sure you can keep it. You may have to break your promise at times. It can happen. Older children may understand and forgive. A younger child will find it much harder to understand. They also find it hard to accept the prospect of "some time soon." Keep your promise and your timing specific.

C H A P T E R 4 0

A "Love Letter" to an In-Law

> *. . . Whither thou goest, I will go;*
> *and where thou lodgest I will lodge.*
> *Thy people shall be my people . . .*
> —Ruth 1:16-17

his thoughts

P ut aside all the jokes about in-laws and face reality. Each marriage consists of six people: the bride, the groom, her parents, and his. If you don't get along with your in-laws, you are casting a huge shadow over your marriage and endangering its chances for survival.

I'm not saying it's easy and, believe me, I have my share of war stories to tell, but I am saying it is important. Look at it this way, you love your wife and they raised her. Odds are she is that special person you adore not in spite of her parents but because of them. They only want what is best for her. So do you. That's a lot to have in common—more than most people have.

Personally, I believe most folks really do like their in-laws and many are the beneficiaries of an awful lot of assistance they get from them—assistance that ranges from baby-sitting to down payments. But even if that's not the case, they are still *family*. Yes, that's right, family. Mom and dad to your wife, grandma and grandpa to your children. Remember that Commandment about honoring your mother and father. Well, I think it applies equally to hers.

Besides, tactically thinking, I'll bet that if you took a moment to drop your in-laws a line, it'd really please your wife. Please her? Dumbfound is more like it.

The following letter is to my ex–father-in-law. I've only known two saints in my life: one is a fellow named Arie Lova Eliav in Israel; the other is Joyce's dad. Read the letter and you'll see why.

ḣis Leꞇꞇer

Dear . . .

It has been a long time since we've seen each other but I'm planning to come down to Florida in a while and I thought I might give you a call and come on over to visit.

I keep in touch with how you and Helen are doing through your daughter. I'm sure you know that we have remained good friends over the years despite the divorce. Why not? You raised one fine daughter.

That's not the only reason I respect you, though. When I think of all the folks I know, I figure you are the best of the lot—and there are some really wonderful people in that lot. Despite your wife's progressive illness over a generation and a half, you've always been there for her—day and night, caring, nursing, nurturing and providing. It's almost as if God gave her a guardian angel of her own to help make up for the tragedy of her affliction.

Many times in my life when things haven't gone as I wished them to, I've thought about her and her life and realized how very fortunate I have been. And other times when I was pretty pleased with myself and thought what a good fellow I was, I've thought about you and your life and realized that I didn't even come close.

You're quite a guy and I have been privileged to know you. And my children have been honored to have you as their grand-father.

I'll call you when I get to town. Love to Grandma.

Sid

ber feelings

"In-laws should be outlawed." That's what you're likely to hear when you're about to get married. The comment is a warning that your spouse's family will cause you trouble.

In-laws are maligned throughout our culture. We somehow imagine that they care only about their own family member, not about the member by marriage. "After all," the popular thinking goes, "in-laws are not your flesh and blood, so they won't care much about you. In fact, they won't even like you. You'll be an outsider, an interloper. They'll wonder "what he sees in you."

But that's all wrong.

O.K. You and your in-laws aren't blood relatives. But there is a word that describes your relationship. That word is "affinal," and it denotes *affinity*. You know that there's an affinity between you and your partner. If there weren't, you never would have gotten together in the first place. There's also an affinity between your partner and his family. That's why he maintains his relation-ship with them. And most likely, his family will find you a likable and lovable extension of him.

Does this mean that all will be smiles between you and your husband's family? Of course not. You don't expect the relationship between the two of you to be without its ups and downs, do you? What's more, every one of us has problems in our individual relationships with our own families—before we ever have a partner. So there's bound to be some tugs and pulls from his family, and from your own. If it is a second marriage or if either one or both of you have children from former marriages, you may walk a pretty tight rope for a while. The previous partner already has space in the family, either fleeting or permanent. You may have some difficulty carving out your own.

In-laws provide you with a whole new network of loving connections, a built-in extended family. If you're lucky, you may get the grandparents you never got a chance to know, the sister or brother you never had. Remember: you and your in-laws love the same person. And that person loves you. Surely you can't all be wrong.

ϩer Lecter

Dear . . .

Thanks for the piano lesson. Maybe one day I'll be able to count time and use my fingers at the same time, but I'd hate to hang till it happens. Oh well, I'd just as soon hear you play anyway.

I should thank you for a lot of things. Like teaching me to sing out loud. Was I ever shy when I was a child. It was hard for me to talk out loud. You and your father cured that the day we visited him when I was ten. You taught me all those old Irish songs: "If I Had My Life to Live Over," "Finnegan, My Wild Irish Rose." Now people ask me if I'll kindly shut up.

You were my brother, something I never had until you married my sister. Your playful affection drew me out of my shell. I was intrigued by your skill in cabinetry and your elegant drawings. You encouraged me in my own and gave me my first real artist's tools.

You were my only "male model" other than my father and an uncle who rarely visited. My idea of a perfect marriage was formed by the way you and my sister related to each other, my image of a perfect home the home you made together.

Later in my life, you gave me good advice and guidance many times. I didn't always follow it—to my regret. You are insightful, thoughtful, and considerate. You are always willing to listen and advise again, to help in whatever way you can when I'm having difficulties, even when you play devil's advocate. You can make me see my role in the problem, recognize my self-deception.

You and my sister gave me faith enough in myself to take charge of my life, to hang on to my house when I was having financial difficulties, to go out on my own, to start my own business. Together, you showed me how to have fun. You taught me much about art and music. You made history come alive for me.

Most important, you taught me that in order not to be bored or boring everyone must have a vital interest all their own, something that demands energy and involvement, something that can't be taken away.

I'm so glad you are part of our family. I'm very lucky to have you for a brother.

Love,
Linda

P.S. | When you write a "love letter" to your in-law:

Do seek out the things you have in common with your in-laws as individual people. They are just that, not merely an extension of your spouse.

Do try hard to maintain cordial relations with your in-laws at all times. Your relationship with your spouse is bound to be better for it.

Do emphasize the closeness of the relationship between your children (if any) with both sets of grandparents. Even strained in-law relationships often improve once in-laws become grandparents.

Don't drag in-laws into any disputes that arise in your marriage. They shouldn't have to choose sides. (Whose side are they likely to choose anyway?)

Don't criticize your spouse to his or her family—or your own, for that matter.

Don't abandon good relationships you achieve with in-laws if your marriage should end. Maintain the contact and your friendship.

C H A P T E R   4 1

A "Love Letter" to a Customer

Civility costs nothing and buys everything.
—Lady Mary Wortley Montagu

ЂIS FEELIПGS

Thank the man for the order!
You want her to order again?
Thank the lady for the order!
There "ain't" no will like goodwill. It's plenty hard to get a customer and real easy to lose one. Why not keep the ones you have? Say thanks for the order.

Say more than thanks if you've a mind to. The manager of the Sheraton Princeville on Kauai sends me a birthday card each year. The owners of The Cliff House in Ogonquit, Maine, send all their guests an annual, folksy newsletter. Mike Damsky, my Allstate agent, drops me a note every so often just to ask how I am. He never mentions insurance; doesn't have to. I once even got a mash note from the telephone company thanking me for paying my bill promptly. I was so impressed I called my son across country to tell him. I figure they made the cost of their stamp back several times over.

his LeTTeR

Dear . . .

I appreciated your recent order and want you to know that we are already moving forward on it. Delivery will not only be on time, it may well be early. I personally intend to watch over every aspect of its fulfillment and, if you have any questions along the way, please feel free to call me collect.

Your loyalty over the years is both a source of pride and a challenge to us to continue to earn your faith. You are the reason we are in business and repeat customers whose accounts are always settled promptly enable us to prosper and to grow.

It truly is our pleasure to serve you.

Sid

her feeLiNgs

No matter what kind of business you're in, the customers or clients on the other side of the counter or desk help set the tone of your work day. A friendly face and interaction makes the business easier, the work lighter. A surly customer can spoil a day quickly.

If you are self-employed as I am, you may do much of your business by phone and mail, seeing your customers seldom. Some you never meet.

Some you are happy not to meet. They are the few who are

abrupt to the point of rudeness, quick to criticize, slow to praise and slower to pay, excessively demanding, imprecise in instruction, overbearing, those who make you feel like a servant, not someone offering a service.

Then there are the "angels," human, warm, and helpful. They are clear in what they expect and issue clear directives. They are courteous, cheerful, and appreciative of your efforts. They are flexible—willing to extend a deadline and allow adequate time to insure good performance. They acknowledge a task well done and give credit where due. They also let you know when a task will be more tedious than usual. Even if you never meet face to face, you have a special feeling of warmth for them, as for a good friend. I'd like to address one of them. Maybe you have a special one in mind yourself.

ÞER LETTER

Dear . . .

Well, you did it again. Your note cracked me up and made the whole job almost bearable. I can always count on you. And thanks for the two-day extension. I've been up to my ears for three weeks now and everything got backed up. Now I can almost see my desk.

Your information about the islands really helped. Now I can plan my vacation better. How nice to have someone who scouts out all the best (and most reasonable) places. But these prices are unbelievable! Who ever heard of $35.00 a day for a seaside room? Are you sure you weren't time-traveling? The last time I went to San Francisco, the room cost $285.00 and I was billed separately for each macadamia nut. You sure pick exotic places, but I think I'll pass on the white-water rafting.

How's good old _____ ? I miss some of the folks. You must be swamped yourself judging from the steady flow of packages

I've been getting from you. I remember how hard it was to juggle all those manuscripts and issues and still keep the editors happy. But I don't think I was ever as calm and collected as you. Never so cheerful and courteous. You always brighten my work day. I look for your note and your little drawings before I check out the package contents.

As soon as I finish this boondoggle, I'll send it back—on time, too. Then I'm off to do some beachcombing. I'll send you a hibiscus flower from Cancun—or whatever else interesting grows there.

P.S. I hope you never leave that job. Don't know what I'd do without you.

Linda

P.S. | When you write a "love letter" to your customer:

Do take the time to let your customers know you appreciate their patronage.

Do keep it light, but make it sincere.

Don't forget: Without your customers, you have no business.

A "Love Letter" to a Boss

Example is always more efficacious than precept.
—Anonymous

ƒeeLIɲƏS

L ove letter to a boss?!! You can't stand your boss. Bosses are tyrants and monsters. The one who grudges you a raise, who neglects to praise, who reneges on a promised promotion, who doesn't acknowledge your presence except to ask for coffee, who takes credit for your ideas, or who drives you crazy. We've all had bosses like that, or a series of bosses above bosses, persons in a penthouse office whom we never see or by whom we are intimidated. There were bosses who were not supportive of us because they were fearful of their own positions or unsure of the scope of their own responsibilities, bosses who bought a scant bouquet of carnations during Secretary's Week, who took us to a yearly sales luncheon, who brought in sandwiches and punch for an abortive office party during the holiday season (after we all chipped in to buy a silver service for him).

But surely you've had one boss who was concerned about the atmosphere of the workplace. One who saw that you had good lighting, functional and comfortable furniture, up-to-date equipment. One who asked for your input, respected your ideas and implemented them, gave you credit. One who was willing to teach and to increase your responsibilities (and pay) as you learned—not to take advantage of you but to help you progress. One who was aware of employees as people, who closed a little early on a stormy day, or who sympathized when unexpected personal crises arose.

We've had a number of bosses combining all the bad elements described above and some medium and good bosses. The best boss we ever had was a super managing editor and the glue that kept a small publishing company going. Because he was immensely capable, extra duties were piled on him. He was underappreciated, overworked, and harried—far too many journals to produce, not enough help, and too many diverse people dependent on him for a final O.K. or guidance in the next project: subeditors and production, sales, and circulation personnel. A line of people loaded down with files and folders always waited by his office door. Somehow, Jim was always calm. He was infallibly courteous, a quintessential gentleman. So everyone brought their disputes to him. Anger dissipated in his presence and the disputes were resolved. He was understanding. So people came to him with their personal problems: no car, no money, no boyfriend. He couldn't solve their problems necessarily, but he listened and comforted. He could and did resolve personality clashes among personnel to a great extent.

Jim only became angry when confronted with something that was either patently unfair or a lie. His anger seemed touched by sadness that someone could behave so badly. But his most outstanding characteristic was tactfulness. He was thorough and exacting, not settling for less than the best. His final product was consistently first rate. He forgot no detail and would not tolerate sloppiness. In order to achieve quality, he used a simple phrase: "Maybe you'd like to take this back to your desk and look it over again." When you caught your own glaring error or minor mistake and corrected it, his comment was mild once more: "Fine, we'll go with that."

We learned a lot from Jim: carefulness, high standards, and recognition of what constitutes a "good" boss. He now runs his own company. We're sure his employees are learning the same things.

LETTER

Dear . . .

Congratulations. I should have written this letter long ago. But I know your journals are off and running and I'm happy to know it. You deserve all the success there is and then some. You certainly helped many others achieve it, although you may not be aware of it. You sure helped me.

After working with you, I worked for three other companies before I decided to go out on my own. It's been going well, in part due to you.

I can tell you now what you probably knew the first day I worked with you: I'd never done book production a day in my life. Advertising, editing, and feature writing were my skills. Enough artwork to know a T-square from a triangle. A good command of English, and the ability to be a "quick study." But not enough to fool you. You never let on. It was your patience and tutelage that carried me through.

Your teaching has stood me in good stead ever since. Before

I sign off on a job, I ask myself: "Is it good enough for Jim?" If the answer is yes, off it goes; if no, I go through the work again. It's a good test.

Please give my best regards to your family and to any of the old staff who are with you. And please accept my thanks. You were the most exacting and demanding boss I ever had—and the fairest and the best.

May you prosper.

Linda

P.S. | When you write a "love letter" to your boss:

Do remind your boss of the specific job and the time your worked for him. Many employees may have come and gone since then.

Do stress the abilities and characteristics that you believe made (and continue to make) your boss such a good boss and a memorable mentor.

Don't effuse. This is not a true "love" letter. It is really a thank-you note.

A "Love Letter" to a Co-Worker

Who is honored?
He who honors others.
　　　　—Ben Zoma, *Ethics of the Fathers*

ḣis ꝺeeliṅgs

I t is important to have a mentor and to have helpful, trusted colleagues who offer guidance and support. The modern business world exists in a highly competitive environment and back-biting or "political" associates only add to job tensions. A supportive, caring co-worker can be a blessing.

And one ought to say thanks for blessings.

his Letter

Dear . . .

I want you to know how very much I appreciate all the help you have given me these past few weeks as I struggled to assume my new responsibilities at work. Settling in is rarely easy but the transition period has gone as well as anyone might expect, largely because of your generous assistance.

It makes me happy to realize what an unselfish, knowledge-able friend I have in the office. The only thing that would make me happier is if sometime I could find the occasion to help you as you have helped me.

We can count on each other—and that's a lot to say in life.

Sid

her feelings

No, we're not suggesting you begin an office affair. They can be uneasy alliances. We are suggesting that you may have someone in your office or workplace who is an unsung hero.

Most of us spend at least half our waking lives in the work-place. Whether we spend that time in a pleasant or tense atmosphere, at ease and companionable or guarded and isolated, depends greatly on our interactions with our co-workers.

Most of us have met the "office gossip" or "informer" in some work situation. This is the person, usually insecure or inefficient, who tries to curry favor with a boss by carrying tales or by denigrating the performance of fellow workers. Luckily, such people are few and far between or are soon history.

Luckily, too, there is usually at least one co-worker who lifts the mood of the office, who promotes friendliness and good will by small gestures: showing newcomers where to keep their coffee mugs, how to work the copier or computer, how to perform a lab technique, advising them of the of the best lunch places in the area. The co-worker may be the maintenance man who keeps your office super slick and escorts you to your car in the parking lot when you work late. She may be the supervisor who helps you understand company policy and protocol, who asks you to join her in the cafeteria at lunchtime, who helps you get a tough job done, and then acknowledges your efforts. Or he may be the manager who places a flower and a welcome note on your desk on your first day. Such co-workers are blessings. People who take the time and effort to welcome newcomers and make them feel comfortable and valued in their jobs are most often capable and hardworking themselves. They understand the complexities of the work situation and realize that newcomers have the potential to become a productive and valued member of a team. They're willing to put themselves out to achieve that end. And they deserve our thanks.

ḥer Letter

Dear . . .

Hi, cookie! How are you? Bet you've got them shaken up in your new job: every wall freshly painted, every file organized, every paper clip lined up, and fresh flowers on every desk. How do you do it?

"I can take care of it." And you certainly can and could. You not only took care of your own work, but you also had time to help everyone else with theirs. Even sour old Mr. B___ would permit himself a smile in your presence.

You were about the only bright light in that uptight place. I found out later that they had the highest turnover rate in the industry—about 70% yearly. No agency in New York will send anyone there to interview. Six months was as long as I could take. After you left, things just got drearier, with a capital D. We missed you sorely.

I wish you great success in your new position. I'm sure you'll have it. And certainly they're lucky to have you. If you don't find them to your liking, come here. We could use your energy and your ability, your thoughtfulness and your cheerful face.

Be well and be happy.

Linda

P.S. When you write your "love letter" to your co-worker:

Do write. We all like to know our efforts are appreciated.

Do tell your co-worker of the specific ways your job has been made easier or more pleasant by the help you've been given.

Don't effuse. Just like your letter to a boss, this is really a thank-you note.

Suggesting an Affair

Gather ye rosebuds while ye may
Old Time is still a' flying . . .
—Robert Herrick, "To the Virgins,
to Make Much of Time"

Gather the Rose of love, whilst yet is time.
—Edmund Spenser, *The Faerie Queene*

ḣis ꝼeeliṇgs

In the best of all possible worlds, every time you loved someone, they'd love you back and you'd both be unattached. Life doesn't work that way. There are times when you fall hopelessly in love with another and either or both of you are not free to live that love openly.

Considering the risks involved, it is almost certain that a love which prompts people to enter into an affair is as intense as love can get. Surely some affairs are reckless and are conducted with an abandonment that guarantees discovery. Others are conducted with circumspection and care. But even in such a case, the parties rarely give sufficient attention to the feelings of others and to the consequences which must inevitably be paid—both by the participants and those they are destined to hurt.

But love is love and to expect that our emotions will always be governed by reason is to ignore what it means to be human. If you must be with her, if you must have her, no amount of naysaying from an outsider will stop you. I know. I've been there.

If, therefore, you are determined to proceed, let me at least caution that putting the suggestion in writing may not be the wisest thing you've ever done. Yet, if you were truly wise, you probably wouldn't be considering an affair to begin with. Besides one can imagine circumstances in which the risk of discovery is not a consideration or, at least, is an acceptable one.

We were sitting next to each other on an airplane going to a business meeting thousands of miles away. We were aware of the possibility of becoming lovers, had in fact discussed it, and as the trip approached realized that it was now or never. I wrote the following letter and handed it to her. She read it slowly and gave it back with a simple nod just before we landed.

We began with a letter. We ended with a letter (Chapter 46). I regret nothing. What good would it do?

ḫis Letter

Dearest . . .

   Alone at last!

   Just a pilot, co-pilot, navigator, several flight attendants and two hundred or so passengers. Still, it's a lot better than the office.

   Flying high. I've been flying high since the moment I first saw you. I remember coming into the office that first day, passing your desk as you smiled, and thinking, "that's the prettiest woman I've ever seen!"

A passing thought and little more until we started working on projects together. I remember the steady stream of creative, practical solutions you came up with and thinking, "that's the brightest woman I've ever worked with!"

Still, just a wonderful working relationship for which I was grateful. I remember, however, the first long conversation after hours, purportedly to prepare for some meeting or other though we were both beginning to know better, and thinking, "this is the most sensitive, feeling woman I've ever known."

When did it become love? I wish I knew for that was a moment I'd hold on to forever. I should have known. It was a feeling I'd never had for anyone else. Oh, yes, I'd said "I love you" before, but if that was love, what is this?

This is real love. This feeling that you are with me, inside of me, at one with me always. Not just in the office but when, at day's end, we go our separate ways. You are with me. The long nights when I am in another's arms. Even then you are with me. The never-ending weekends surrounded by friends whose mindless chatter I can no longer bear, then too you are with me.

This is real love. This feeling of absolute joy whenever I see you. Not being able to pass a phone in the street without calling to hear your voice. Learning to appreciate so many simple, wonderful things in life I'd never even seen before until I looked at them through your eyes. The wonder that someone loves me just for who I am, not for what I am—that all you want is my time and nothing more.

This is real love. It is a love that is aware of the consequences for us both, yet persists. Huge consequences, yet persists. We cannot ignore those consequences yet must not allow our love to be thwarted by them. Whatever we are, cowards we are not.

I'd like to think that even had we come into each other's life in perfect happiness, we'd have fallen in love. But I am grateful

273

that whatever the circumstance, we found each other. Grateful because, quite literally, I had stopped feeling until you came into my life. Born so many years before you, I was reborn because of you.

The next few days belong to us. They must belong to us. I feel as if my whole life has been one long journey to you and to this place and to these days. I want you more than anyone or anything I've ever wanted. This is our chance to see if what we have is strong enough, alive enough to bind us together forever, no matter what. We must make the best of that chance.

> *"There is a tide in the affairs of men,*
> *Which, taken at the flood, leads on to fortune . . .*
> *And we must take the current when it serves,*
> *Or lose our ventures."**

Now, my darling, now.

                                        Sid

ђer ₣eeₗiₙgs

Times have changed. Women today are free to make the first move: to be first to call, to suggest a date, to insist on sharing expenses. We are even free to take it further, to suggest sexual involvement. It's chancy, though. Times never change all that much; they just revolve. Certain men are flattered by being approached overtly. Others may be threatened or turned off by what they perceive as an aggressive woman. Be pretty sure of your reception before you make any overture.

There may be several reasons for making the first move. He may be shy and slow to intimacy. He may want to be the initiator, yet has a slower timetable than your own. He may not be sure of his own reception if he makes further advances. He may have

* *The Tragedy of Julius Caesar*, Act IV scene III, by William Shakespeare.

compunctions about sex he hasn't voiced: health related, ethical, or religious. Nevertheless, you're sure he likes your company. He increasingly includes you in his plans and activities. You've met his friends, family, and co-workers. He's indicated affection: kissing, hugging, caressing your hair, draping his arm around you.

He introduces you as his girlfriend. Why doesn't he go further? You can ask, gently or bluntly. You are now placing yourself in what historically has been a man's position or purview, and it's a vulnerable one. You risk rejection or rebuff at worst. At best, you may have relieved him of his own fears, timidity, or reluctance to press forward. And you know where you stand.

If you're fairly sure he is just shy, you can be direct as you wish. If you're not so sure of his reaction, keep your letter light. Leave the door open for more gradual progress. You're not just proposing a roll in the hay and wouldn't want that kind of proposal yourself. You want a deeper and committed involvement.

hER LEttER

Dear . . .

I guess I'm pretty conventional, no matter how much I try to convince myself otherwise. I talk a good story as long as I'm talking to myself, but it's hard to put yourself on the line. It took me two nights to work up my courage to write this letter.

I've wanted to make love with you—from the beginning. From the way you kissed me last night, I'm sure you want to as well.

There! I said (wrote it). And I'm glad.

And by the way, if you think I'm aggressive, drop by tonight about seven, and I might prove you right.

And then . . . I hope you will want to stay—and stay—and stay.

Love,
Linda

P.S. | When you suggest an affair:

Do consider your relationship with the person. You should have reason to believe that your suggestion may be welcome. You can't be sure, but you shouldn't be shooting wild.

Do take a chance. You may not succeed, but if you have the feeling your suggestion might be welcomed, the chance is worth taking.

Do leave the door open. You can be direct or indirect in your proposal and still indicate that you are aware the other person is either not in a position to accept or isn't quite ready to do so.

Do recognize the fact that the answer you receive may be a flat no.

Don't persist if you are turned down flat. Accept the refusal gracefully.

Don't be dishonest. Inform the person of the nature of the relationship you are seeking. If it is an affair you propose, say so. If you are seeking a relationship, say so.

You're with Another, But
You Belong to Me

*If by me broke, what Fool is not so wise
To break an oath, to win a paradise?*
—Shakespeare, *The Passionate Pilgrim,* III

ᚼᛁꟅ ꟻᛖᛖᛚᛁᛝꟅ

t's a good thing to have high hopes, but let's be realistic: "An ant can't move a rubber tree plant." If another's relationship is firmly rooted and sufficiently nourished, chances are that any attempt to interfere with its development will be useless. It will also make you feel, and appear, awfully silly. It can have disastrous consequences for your reputation as well. Bulldozers, it is true, effectively knock down, but the effect of their actions is not always appreciated and, in any case, rebuilding is generally accomplished by someone else.

Yet there are those instances when one romance either starts or picks up again as another is ending. The object of your affections may be involved in a relationship that has either plateaued or is unwinding. You may even care for someone whose current social situation is destructive. You can't help but notice their unhappiness and want to reach out and comfort. At a given time, you may be dating someone who is also seeing another. Such situations call for particular thoughtfulness and discretion. You owe it both to yourself and to the other person to let your feelings be known. Frequently he or she will be pleased to know they have options and aren't "locked in " to a bad or, at least, unrewarding relationship. If you are afraid to speak up, your golden chances may pass you by, as Billy the Barker in *Carousel* feared. Of course, if you speak up too aggressively, you may be seen as trying to take unfair advantage—of being nothing more than an interloper.

Whenever I have faced this problem, I have chosen to take my chances with directness. If I care deeply about someone, I want them to know it. They are then free to make their choice, but I've had the opportunity to put my feelings on the line. It's simply not my style to wait it out or to live a fantasy, "if only she were mine," existence. Quiet desperation doesn't suit me. Of course, I run the risk of rejection, but unless you are willing to be rejected you cannot reasonably anticipate being rewarded. To put it another way, you have to be willing to experience great pain if you would experience great joy , for frequently they are opposite sides of the same coin.

Here is an example of the letters I have written when the person I deeply cared for was involved with another. Sometimes it has worked, sometimes it hasn't. But I've never had to wonder, "What if . . . ?"

hิs Letter

Dear . . .

I am trying so very hard to do the right thing but I am not absolutely sure what that is.

You have been open and honest with me about your relationship with S_____ and I appreciate your candor. I've listened to you tell me of its strengths and weaknesses. I've listened to you tell me how hard he is trying. I've listened to you say that he truly loves you, as I am sure he must. And I have listened hard.

But listen as I might, there is one thing I've never heard you say. You have never said that you love him. Had you said that, I would have wished you well and retreated. I have no intention of interfering with another's happiness.

Not having heard those words, I have continued to ask you out and you have continued to accept (albeit only during the week). The times we have spent together have been wonderful—not necessarily because of the things we have done, rather because of who we are with one another. A magnetic electricity is generated as soon as we meet that positively energizes us. We are so obviously drawn to one another. Just see how we rush to share thoughts, feelings, insights, and reactions. There is a vibrancy when we are together. I have never felt so alive with anyone else.

Something special is happening to us. It's more than closeness. We want to be with each other. You know that and so do I. If your relationship were what it ought to be, if it was sufficiently fulfilling and rewarding, you wouldn't be making time for me—for us. But, thank Heaven, you are. And no matter how circumspect we have been, you are not just another friend of mine, nor I of yours. Keeping my feelings in check has been just about the most difficult thing I've ever done.

I want to take you in my arms and hold you close and talk to you about a future—our future. I believe in that, you see. We seem to fit so well together. We need the same togetherness, we need the same space. We view the world through the same pair of eyes. We share the same perspective, the same understanding.

Each of us is, of course, responsible for our own lives. For my part, I want more—I want all—of you and, in return, am willing to give you all of me. You have to decide what you want and who you want, and when.... There are no ultimatums here. I love you and I'll hold on as long as I can. I just don't know how long that will be.

Yesterday was his. I understand that. Let all the tomorrows be ours.

Sid

hER FEELINGS

No one really "belongs" to anyone else. Nevertheless, you may believe that you have had one special love in your life, a relationship that was never equaled and can never be. You never felt such closeness, such intimacy with anyone else. He was your best friend, your best lover; you still feel you *belong* together.

Nonetheless, the two of you separate. Life gets in the way: timing is wrong, schools or jobs distance you from each other, you have a major fight that you just can't resolve, or he has done something you can't forgive. But when you let him go, the special feelings don't leave with him. In fact, they become stronger.

It's easy to keep your perfect partner—in your mind, that is. Reality can't intrude there. The sex is always great, the touch always loving. His hairline doesn't recede, and his waistline doesn't thicken. There are no dirty socks on the floor, no wet towels on the bed. He's as marvelous as he once was. What's more, you are too, as long as you leave everything right where it is. And maybe you should.

Reaching into the past can be ticklish, even downright dangerous. Before you attempt to do so, ask yourself some questions. Are you fantasizing having contact with your past love because you are dissatisfied with your present partner or want to make him jealous? Bad move. Your present partner may become a past partner in a big hurry. Is your old love free to respond to you? You don't have the right to interfere with the equilibrium of someone else's relationship, no matter what emotions are driving you. Will your old love welcome your renewed interest? No matter what you feel, he may not remember you as the love of his life.

You shouldn't write this letter unless you believe it won't rock anyone's boat, including your own. Tread very softly. And be prepared for the possibility that you will be disappointed.

her Letter

Dear . . .

I ran into Beth last week, and she told me she had seen you a month ago at the theater. She said you looked great and were happy in your new job. I didn't want to let her go. I wanted to hear more about you. She did tell me one other thing: that you weren't alone.

We haven't seen each other for two years, but I haven't been able to forget you. Even though I've dated several men in that time, I find that we don't get past the friendship stage.

Meeting Beth brought back so many memories, our weekend in Martha's Vineyard, our vacation in Montreal, our stay in the cottage in Southampton. I wonder if you remember those times fondly.

I still feel that our relationship was special and that it shouldn't have ended when it did. I must admit that part of me hoped to hear that you were all by yourself and pining for my return. So much for fantasy. I have no way of knowing what your feelings are or what your life is like now. If you are not truly involved with anyone, I would love to hear from you. And if you are involved with someone, I wish you both happiness.

Linda

P.S. When you write to someone you love who is currently involved with another:

Do be careful. You don't want to get shot.

Do be sure of your feelings. You may be exaggerating them or you may have faulty perception or a faulty memory. Remember: When you want something badly enough, you're likely to get it.

Do phrase your letter carefully. Just because you feel the other person ought to be at your side, you can't presume that your feelings are reciprocated. He or she may be quite content in an existing relationship.

Don't make waves. If your first letter gets a poor reception, don't write again. Back off.

Don't take it too hard if you don't succeed.

Ending an Affair

Though nothing can bring back the hour
Of splendour in the grass, or glory in the flower,
We will grieve not, rather find
Strength in what remains behind.
      —William Wordsworth, "Ode to Duty"

his feelings

Perhaps every person who has ever been involved in one says, "It was more than a mere affair." I know it was. Through all the years since, I have measured each new love by how I felt about her. She taught me how to love; she set the standard.

The timing was terrible. Had I met her just a few years before, or just a few thereafter, I truly believe my search would have ended. But then we were both married. The time we had was stolen time. The love we gave was stolen love.

She wanted an "us." I felt compelled to give my failing

marriage one last try. It was a decision I have never regretted though the effort was unsuccessful and it cost me her. In my last letter, I tried to get her to understand that ending what we had did not mean I had stopped loving her. It was just that sometimes love is not enough.

Years later I learned that her marriage had also dissolved. I tried to find her but to no avail. It's just as well. We hurt each other, we hurt others. Castles can't be built on sand. Successful relationships, like great buildings, must rest on solid foundations.

ḣıs Leᴄᴄer

Dearest . . .
  The Word.
  In the beginning was the Word.
  Before the apple was the Word.
  And the Word was No. And the Word was Never.
  No, you mustn't.
  Never must you.
  No, you mustn't say it.
  Never must you say it.
  The Word.
  The Word destroys.
  Other people's marriages.
  Other people's lives.
  Not even whispered, never even thought.
  But the Word is felt, or else
  There is no feeling.
  Only numbers, only stones.
  If I can only feel it, never say it,
  How will she know?
  If I can't tell her,

Must never tell her,
How. . .how will she know?
Know.
Know is the Word.
Know that I love her.
Know that I need her.
Know that I long for her.
"Know."
"Know" is the Word.
No.
"No" is the Word.

Was it wrong for me to tell you that I loved you—that first night across a candlelit table? Those feelings had been building up within me for such a long time. My heart was exploding with the joy of discovery. I had never known anyone like you. All my life had been spent preparing for, struggling for, seeking financial success. I sat in the first pew in Mamon's church. Suddenly there you were, radiating youth, buoyant with happiness, deriving joy from life's simplest pleasures. You made me feel young and carefree and I had never been either.

How could I not tell you? Tell you that I had been blind and you taught me to see: cherry blossoms heralding spring's arrival, lovers strolling casually around the mill basin, children jumping rope rhythmically, an old man carefully removing a speck from the eye of his beloved. Tell you that you taught me to hear: the robin's song, the rustle of leaves, your breath in my ear as we became one. Tell you that my spirit had been moribund and you taught me to feel and not be afraid to express those feelings.

And you taught me something else. The meaning of ecstasy. Whatever lovemaking had been before, it wasn't what you and I shared. You brought me outside myself. I floated, lingered, danced with angels. With you it became a prayer of thanksgiving that we had found each other. The memory of our times together will keep me warm my whole life through.

Thus I said "love" and I meant "love," and saying it gave it a reality and we acted on that reality. But what kind of reality was that—without bills to pay, children to nurse through a fevered night, repairs to make? It was all just a dream. . . but no matter how lovely the dream, I could not rest easy.

For you taught me to see and I saw the anguish on your face as we parted and the disbelief on hers when I returned home.

For you taught me to hear and I heard the lies we told them to protect our stolen moments.

For you taught me to feel and I felt ashamed for compromising you and dishonoring myself.

I cannot go on this way nor can I let you do so. He was your love before you knew me. You were happy once. Be happy again. She was my love since childhood. The sages have written that when a man puts aside the bride of his youth, even the angels cry. I must try again.

Never shall I forget you. Not for one moment of one day. I may regret many things in years to come, but I will never regret having known you.

Know that even though for us the word is "no," your name will be inscribed on my heart forever.

Sid

ḣER FEELIṄGS

Sometimes a relationship flattens out or evaporates, for one or both of you. It can happen after a brief courtship or a long relationship. It doesn't have to be a cataclysm. There may not even seem to be any good reason why the interest, the feeling of oneness, the good feelings are gone.

It may happen because we have moved too quickly. Have you ever said, "He's so different from the way he used to be?" Or, "She's not the person I once knew?" Usually the person hasn't changed at all. But traits we first admired in each other when we first met are no longer so admirable after a while: Attentiveness has become possessiveness, easy-going now appears to be lack of ambition. Sometimes we have changed and the things we now want as part of our lives are not what our partners want for themselves or want for us or in us.

It may happen because we have been pretending, so anxious to become one with someone we love and desire that we abandoned our own wishes and desires—our selves. The self can't stay submerged if a relationship is going to be healthy, open, and satisfactory.

Love affairs, if they are *affairs,* usually have a built in self-destruct button. The old song "Darling, You Can't Love Two" isn't off the mark. You're surely in a stew. It's hard to share your lover with someone else. You spend a lot of time alone. You never really have a life together and you can't experience the pleasure of sharing your lives with others. You must keep your secret. Some few affairs have "happy endings"; that is, two, three (or four) protagonists end up together, delighted, happy, and right for each other. More often, they don't, and all players and spectators end up wounded. If you are involved in a love affair that won't quit or die, it will stand a separation that allows both of you to end other relationships as painlessly as possible. Love develops better in an open free atmosphere.

It's always hard to end an affair, sometimes anguishing. But trying to bolster a failing affair is still more painful. Once you've decided to end it, be brief and final. If there really hasn't been much between you, the letter may be easy to write and easily accepted. But if your affair has been one of real passion and feeling, it will be very hard to write. So be as brief and merciful as possible. Remember the good things and add them in. No one likes being rejected, no matter what the reason. Stick to the facts and the circumstances. Don't place blame—or at least accept your share. Don't recriminate. Bad words and feelings have a way of coming home to roost. Last, don't waver with a lot of "if onlys"; be firm and final. Nothing is quite as painful as jerking back and forth like a yo-yo on a string.

ђer Leccer

Dear . . .

Part of me doesn't want to write this letter. It's off somewhere whimpering and protesting, saying no. But I'm not listening. I'm saying goodbye.

We've made a mistake. We're together for the wrong reasons. Neither one of us is free. You've been separated for a year but can't bring yourself to sue for divorce. I'm still one of the "walking wounded," divorced but not yet over it.

Do you realize that we spend most of our time together talking about our individual past lives and not our present life together? I wonder what we would share if we weren't so busy exchanging pain. Whatever that might be, we'll never discover it until we make peace with the past. In your case, the past is still very much part of the present, at least legally.

I empathized with you when we first met. Your story is so much like my own. But that commonality is not foundation enough for us to build a relationship. We're not whole yet.

We've stayed in this holding pattern for a year now. It's time we moved on with our lives and we'll never do it unless we separate. Make up your mind. Get a divorce or go back to your wife and see if you can work it out between you. Making your decision is going to be easier if I am not in the picture. And whatever you decide, I wish you well.

Linda

P.S. | When you write to end an affair:

Do be gentle. Whatever your reasons for ending an affair,you have residual feelings for the person. No want to be rejected, no matter the circumstances, and whether or not you ever meet again, you both want to keep good memories of your love and each other.

Do be brief. The swiftest cut is the kindest cut.

Do be final. What's done is done.

Don't emphasize the negative. It's over. There's no need to discuss any of the reasons for the failure of the relationship.

C H A P T E R 4 7

A Letter to the Unattainable Lover

Love seeketh not his own! Dear, you may take
My happiness to make you happier,
Even though you never know I gave it to you—
Only let me hear sometimes, all alone,
The distant laughter of your joy!
—Edmond Rostand, *Cyrano de Bergerac*

ber feelings

You are ready for the big "C." You've finished school. You're satisfied with your work and the way in which you've achieved you goals so far. You've had a number of partners, some fairly long term. But you weren't ready then for a real commitment or enough basic elements were lacking for you to know that it wasn't a lifetime involvement; you separated amicably. You even maintained a friendship or a degree of closeness with them.

A year ago, you met Sean, two years older, stable and steady. He is also established in his chosen path. Because your relationship progressed so well, you moved into his apartment and have lived together on a trial basis for six months. The first four months of "playing house" were wonderful. You bought some furniture you both liked, new dishes, a new refrigerator. He said he liked the new hominess. You loved the idea of being together in a more permanent way; in fact, you felt almost married. But the last two months have been a real *trial*. You don't want to play any more. You want a wedding and he suddenly has more than cold feet. He seems cold all over.

You met Joel two years ago. He is a Jew. You are gentile. He regularly attends temple and observes the high holidays. You are devoted to your religion and similarly take part in church activities. This played no significant role in the early part of your relationship. What did religion have to do with your strong attachment to each other? That could be dealt with in time. It's time. You have discussed marriage. You have one insurmountable barrier. Neither of you wants children raised in another religion except your own—and you both want children.

You and David have been a "thing" for almost five years. You have lived together for three; although you still keep your separate residences, you live together, for the most part, in both of them. You even have a joint bank account. People usually assume you are married. Yet every time you've pushed to go the final step, he makes the same responses. "Don't fix something that isn't broken." "Why invite the State into our relationship?" "It's perfect as it is. In fact, it's better than marriage. We're both in it because we want to be, not because we have to be. Marriage makes divorce." At two years, even three years, that was O.K. with you. You weren't so sure yourself. Now you question whether your relationship is stagnant. Whether you might not as well have marriage benefits as long as you're "acting" the part of a marriage partner. How long is long enough? Too long?

Before you write your letter, assess the situation as coolly as possible. First be sure that you want to issue an ultimatum. Are you willing to end the relationship if you can't reach an agreement on marriage? Are there promises or compromises that you would accept—a future date or a commitment to a date in the near future? Have any of your own fears of being able to commit kept you in a holding position?

If you believe that the relationship can't continue, why hold on? Get on with your separate lives.

hER LETTER

Dear . . .

I've loved you for four years. I've been your "wife" for three. Without bell, book, or candle. Without portfolio.

This is a hard, hard letter to write. I threw out seven drafts before I wrote this one. I think it will be hard for you to accept and I am sorry.

With this letter is your ring, the ring that was never quite a symbol of anything. You know I'm not much more of a romantic than you are. But I wore your ring for two years, persuading myself like some twelfth-grader that it meant you were committed to me.

We are poles apart now. Maybe we always were and I just wouldn't admit it. We stopped building anything at least a year ago. I don't know what your reluctance is, what fear you can't overcome, why you have fostered this stalemate. We don't talk. We don't say much more to each other than "pass the butter."

We've already lived together longer than some couples stay married. I once hoped I would have a child by the time I was thirty. Now I've upped the age to forty. I know it will not happen with you. You are nowhere near ready to be a husband, much less a father.

Even a month ago, I couldn't have written this letter. I wasn't

293

ready. I wasn't ready to let go of the good things we have had together. But now I must let go. We must be done with this so that we both may have a chance with someone else, a new love, a new life. I've waited and hoped too long.

Goodbye,

Linda

P.S. | When you write to an unattainable lover:

Do emphasize how much your relationship has meant to you. You are separating because you realize you have no realistic possibility of a future together. Until recently, your past has been good.

Don't waver. You will both endure far more anguish if you postpone the inevitable breakup.

A Letter of Unrequited Love

But for iron the magnet felt no whim
Though he charmed iron, it charmed not him . . .
*   this magnetic*
Peripatetic
Lover he lived to learn,
By no endeavour
Can magnet ever
Attract a Silver Churn.

—Gilbert and Sullivan, *Patience*

ÐER FEELINGS

ou love him! It's marvelous! He doesn't love you. Anguish. Anyway, no go. If love is to be, it must be reciprocal, and if this world were perfect, everyone we loved would love us back—and to the same degree. Alas, the world isn't perfect and they don't. There's nothing worse or more unproductive than crying in your pillow or your beer over what isn't and can't be yours. The question to ask yourself is whether you really do or can love someone who doesn't love you.

You did everything you could to make him notice you. You changed your hair style and color, your clothes. You bought him cards and little gifts on any and every occasion. You helped him paint his dorm room, you helped him research his term paper. In fact, you've knocked yourself out. You feigned interest in his activities: you learned to bowl and watched football games even though you hate sports. You invited him to parties or dinners. He came once or twice, but accepted halfheartedly: It was just enough to strengthen your feelings and fuel your belief that he has the same ones.

He may be your boss, co-worker, teacher, or neighbor. You interpreted a friendly act or comment as growing interest and concern. He praised you when you landed an account, he brought you candy when he noticed birthday cards on your desk, he gave you extra help on an independent study project, he took in your packages or helped set up your stereo system. What else could it be but love? Why else would he show you so much attention? He's in your thoughts every minute now. You wait at home in the hope that he'll call. You frequent places you think he might be. You exaggerate every small favor or remark as a sign of his growing love, studiously ignoring the fact that he doesn't ask you out, that he shows no real interest in developing friendship past these minor involvements.

What a waste. If you were devoting all these energies and effort to your own interests, you might be a better piano player or painter, a notch higher in your job, a better friend. You might be encountering (at least not overlooking) someone who shares your interests and will have reciprocal feelings. Unwanted attentions won't make someone love you, and they may lose you someone who could be a good friend.

You're about to write another love letter you won't send. Pour out your passion in all its intensity. Also describe every act, behavior, or gesture he has made. Write down every word you remember him speaking. Are they anywhere near equal? Probably not even close. You can't fabricate love or manipulate someone into loving you by the strength of your own feelings or by parading them. Try to imagine yourself as the recipient of unwanted attentions. Acknowledge your exaggeration of his interest in you, your fantasy "love," and the futility of your endeavor. Writing this letter is a learning experience. Hang on to it. You'll laugh at it someday (or be embarrassed) when you find real love.

ҺER LETTER

Dear . . .

I love you so. How could you ignore love like mine? It can overcome all barriers, all obstacles. I would never let you down. I can never give you up. You mean the whole world to me.

From the minute I saw you, I was lost. I could see no other face than yours. When you began to notice me, I was overjoyed. You spoke to me in the hall. You shared soap with me in the laundry room. You brought me a quart of milk when I couldn't get out to the store. You walked my dog for me the day I was home sick. I can't believe you would have done all that for me if you didn't love me.

There's nothing about you I don't love: your voice, your walk, the blue of your eyes, the set of your shoulders. I feel as though I know everything about you even though we have never been together for more than five minutes at a time. I listen for the sound of your footsteps every evening and pray you will stop at my door. Please know how much I love you. I will never love another for the rest of my life. Don't let me love in vain.

Forever yours,
Linda

P.S. | When you tell your tale of unrequited love:

Do write the letter. It will help you see the futility of your unrequited love. It will also help you recognize your misconceptions and misperceptions. It is a learning device. It will help prevent you from making a complete fool of yourself.

Do remember this: Whatever you do, DON'T MAIL the letter!!

CHAPTER 49

A Letter to an Ungrateful Lover

> *Love—all that it has brought me . . .*
> one kiss and twenty kicks in the ass.
> —Voltaire, *Candide*

ꜧER ꜰEELIꞄGS

S ometimes you try hard and long to maintain a relationship. But an unequal or painful relationship, even one that is just not much fun, is not worth maintaining. You may have prolonged it for any number of reasons: fear of being alone, of starting the search again, of losing the time and effort you've invested. You may feel you just haven't worked hard enough, haven't given enough, haven't accommodated enough. But you know that you aren't happy, that you don't really look forward to being in his company. In fact, you feel pretty miserable. He no longer asks you what you would like to do. Neither does he like your suggestions. He is hypercritical of you and often impatient. He doesn't like your friends or want to spend any time with them. He doesn't particularly seem to enjoy spending time with you, but he doesn't want you to go anywhere without him. He says you nag him and complain, that you're not as much fun as you used to be. You've almost begun to believe him. Sometimes you wonder whether you're worth loving.

It's time to take stock. Are you guilty of any of his accusations? Are you guilty of any of his actions? Are there any aspects of your relationship that make it worth preserving? Is he just insensitive and unused to being half of a couple? Uncomfortable with expressing tenderness? Is he from a culture or background in which men are supposed to be strong, silent, and authoritative? Or is he just a creep?

If creep it is, it's time to write a love letter. *Love letter?* Yes. This one's to you and for you. You are in a relationship that is sapping your energy, your happiness, and your self-esteem. Pick up your pen and tell him so and let him go. It's time to look for love.

ḥER LETTER

Dear . . .

We've had some fun together, but lately not much. You don't like to be with my friends and you don't want to share my activities. When you do, on occasion, you seem almost pained. These things are vital to my life and I hoped to share them with you. Perhaps I wouldn't mind not sharing them if we enjoyed a lot of other things together. Many "opposites" attract and stay attracted. We are pulling apart, not together.

I have become very careful about how I act when I am with you. I catch myself censoring my words, even my thoughts. I watch your face to gauge your reactions to what I finally say aloud. I find

300

myself telling friends that I'll have to check with you before I make any plans. I'm losing my edges. Beginning to define myself by what you say, what you say you see in me, as though you were my mirror. And it's not such a great image reflected in your eyes. I don't like it. And it isn't me.

I have tried several times to tell you of my feelings. My dissatisfaction with our relationship is registered as nagging. My suggestions for ways we might improve our time together are termed complaints. I wonder what you'll think of this letter.

Actually, I don't care much. But I do wish you well. I do wish you a new relationship. And I hope you'll handle it better, more tenderly, and with more respect.

Goodbye,
Linda

P.S. When you write to an ungrateful lover:

Do evaluate your relationship. Be honest. Reconsider its positive and negative qualities and those of your partner—and your own.

Don't hedge. Be specific about your reasons for ending your relationship. The knowledge may help your present partner attain and maintain a healthy relationship with someone else.

Don't hesitate.

Don't pull your punches. End it!

On a Birthday

Because the birthday of my life
Is come, my love is come to me.
　　　　—Christina Rossetti, "A Birthday"

his feelings

Birthdays are big events for some people—and I'm one of them. I go all out to make the day special for those who are special to me. (See Chapter 58, "The Three-Dimensional Love Letter.") I know Washington, Lincoln, and Dr. King's birthdays are important events but I have to tell you they are not as important to me as "her" birthday—whoever she might be. And, I admit, I just love it when friends make a fuss over me on my birthday. Inside of every man there really is a little boy.

There are those, I am sure, who would just as soon forget birthdays—or say they would anyway. I believe everyone likes to be remembered and a birthday is an absolutely wonderful opportunity to tell someone you care for, "I'm glad you are here. I'm glad you are you."

I'm not a pack rat but I've saved most of the birthday (and Valentine) cards and letters I've received over the years. When I'm down, I like to read them and remember. In a way, they are a continuing gift—a lot better than another necktie. (Although if you pass the Bijan or Pauline Trégère collection before next May 3 . . .)

On my last birthday I received a very brief note from "my son, the lawyer." It has become one of my most prized possessions.

> *For all the support, encouragement and advice you give me in everything I do . . . and for the example you set for me in everything you do—you deserve the best birthday anyone ever had!*
>
> *You continue every day to be my best friend as well as my Dad. I appreciate everything . . . and I love you.*

I think sending a birthday letter is much more meaningful than merely sending a birthday card. After all, that scribe in Kansas City doesn't know your sweetheart at all. Those greeting card sentiments might give you ideas, just the way this book will give you ideas. But it is only when you add the gift of self, when you express your own feelings, that the message truly becomes important.

If you really want her to know how much you care, take the time to carefully compose a loving birthday letter. Its significance will be heightened on that day as on no other. Andra used to write me birthday poems. I still miss them.

The most important person in my life will celebrate her birthday in just two days. She'll find the following letter in her mailbox that morning.

his Letter

Dearest . . .

Next to Valentine's Day, which gives me a chance to celebrate how much I love you, your birthday is my favorite holiday. On this day I celebrate your very existence. So happy, happy birthday, my cherished one. The world is quite simply a better place, and everyone who knows you a better person, because you were born thirtysomething years ago.

You've already received your gift. It was too pretty, and I too impulsive, to keep it in my drawer awaiting this day. But birthdays call for gifts on the day and what have I left to give you? I give you this:

My friendship when you need a friend, constant and abiding.

My love for as long as I live, faithful and true.

My understanding, no matter what arises, that I may be your safe harbor.

My support in every way that one person can help another.

My concern so you will know that somewhere there is always one who cares.

My devotion for you may always count on me.

My tolerance for you are your own person and are not here to please me.

My sincerity because I know you trust me.

My laughter so you may share my joy.

My experience that you may, if you choose, benefit from it.

My compassion so I may better appreciate your feelings.

My tenderness to care for and protect you through all that life may have in store.

*A dozen verbal roses, my birthday bouquet to you. A dozen.
One for every thousand times I think of you. One for every million
times I love you.*

Happy birthday, sweetheart. Happy, happy birthday.

Sid

her feelings

Sixteen candles. What a great year that was! But as the candles
begin to obscure more and more of the surface of your birthday
cakes, you may opt to use only three: one each for yesterday,
today, and tomorrow. Maybe one more for good luck or to ward
off the evil eye. A konnehurra candle. You may decide to ignore
your birthdays completely or at least give up the cake. To shave
a few years off the age you'll admit to. To celebrate every day as
a gift, not just birthdays.

Are you the kind who delights at being given a surprise party?
Would you be thrilled if a waiter carried out a blazing cake as the
climax of a birthday dinner in your honor? You're Type A. Do you
cringe in embarrassment at such display? Do you wish the whole
matter could be dispensed with, ignored? You're Type B. No big
deal. Only when Type A and Type B merge do problems arise. But
the problems don't have to be a big deal. Just a little annoyance,
a minor pain in the neck. Type A can hint and nudge for months
in advance of a birthday, making suggestions about the way she
would like to spend her special day, the gift she would like to have.
(Most of us give and hope to receive gifts, and we expect the
suggestion will be reasonable and suitable to circumstances.)
Type B can learn to accept that birthdays are meaningful to others
even if they are nothing much to him. In time, he may decide he
likes them himself, or that he likes Type A to make just a little fuss
on his day. My father viewed birthdays and similar occasions as

profit opportunities for greeting card manufacturers. His scorn increased yearly. "Look at that! 'Happy Halloween to a Great Great-Aunt!' What next? 'Congratulations on Your Release from Prison' ?" Nevertheless, he had a great fondness for angelfood cake and never refused one. And recently, my mother showed me some of his earliest cards to her before their marriage, some "homemade," some with poetry, all sentimental .

You may be able to afford a diamond necklace for your sweetheart, a set of golf clubs for your lover. You may have no money at all for a gift. Let your gift be a small token then, an offer to do the chores for the day, to perform one he or she actively dislikes. Cook a special meal, serve breakfast in bed, make a cake or buy a cupcake. And write a love letter to say how glad you are that your partner's present birthday is spent with you, and that each future one will be another important milestone for you as well.

hER LETTER

Dear . . .

Where were you on the night of December 31, 1950—getting born, of all things. What a way to greet the New Year. And what a lucky day for me. I didn't know it though.

Just think how many years went by, how many candles we blew out separately to get to today's cake. How many miles to get to this place. How many people.

I wish I could have seen you when you were 2, 10, 16, 21. I wish I had celebrated every one of your birthdays with you. And I want to help you celebrate every one from now on.

Years, miles, people have separated us until now—all past and irretrievable. I write this Happy Birthday letter for todays and tomorrows. "Cent' anni!" May you have another hundred birthdays and may I be there at every one to say "I love you."

Linda

P.S. | When you write a birthday love letter:

Do take your partner's birthday seriously even if you don't give a hoot aboutyour own. Your letter will be a cherished gift for many birthdays to come.

Do be imaginative. Include a newspaper complete with headline announcement of your partner's birth (handmade or available from specialty printers), a gilt-edged copy of your partner's birth certificate, a crossword puzzle in which every definition will call for the word love, a dot-to-dot drawing that when connected will illustrate a happy face, or a pay-on-demand check entitling your partner to a service you promise to perform (you pick the service you'd love to render).

Don't forget even if you must tie strings around all your fingers. Your remembering may bring you all sorts of love in return.

On an Anniversary

Could we but relive that one moment sublime,
We'd find that our love is unaltered by time.
—Al Jolson, "The Anniversary Song"

his feelings

Whether it is a wedding anniversary or simply the anniversary of the day you met, such occasions present true cause for celebration. The complexity of everyday life, the stressesand tensions it produces, the alternatives and opportunities which a mobile society present, makes sustaining any relationship difficult. When a couple has managed to survive the "slings and arrows of outrageous fortune," and grow and develop together, even the angels in Heaven must rejoice.

Anniversary love letters are, I think, my favorites for the

feelings they express are founded on hard-won experience. It is one thing to ask someone to climb a mountain with you and quite another to have climbed it together. That's the time to pause and to reflect and, as the Roman God Janus, look backward and forward at the same time.

After all their years together, Teyve still asked Golde, "Do you love me?" Anniversaries are a wonderful time to answer the question.

Perhaps I'm a little sentimental about anniversaries because we didn't have enough of them.

his Letter

Dearest . . .

This hand was steadier when we were younger but the words, I think, not quite so worthwhile. Oh, I do remember courting you with prose and poetry alike, some my own and some borrowed, but they were designed merely to gain your favor and to impress. These words are like the gray hairs that now adorn my head—the result of living, of experiencing, and of surviving. I've got your favor now, have had it for all the years leading up to this anniversary—and it's too late to impress. You've seen the truth as no other. No, now I can simply tell it straight.

I loved you when I first saw you and have loved you more each passing day. In fact, the love I have for you now is so much richer, so much deeper than what we first knew, it bears precious little resemblance. Then we were still new—to the world and to each other. It was all going to be ours and it was all going to be easy. How soon we learned!

Yet, through it all, birth and death, success and failure, early morning and late night, we survived. No, more than survived. We grew. I know we grew because the heart I had then was not large enough to contain the love I have for you now nor was my soul large enough to contain the appreciation. You stuck by me, right there by me, as the winds of fortune tossed us about. Sometimes I can still feel your hand in mine though we be separate for the moment.

You were the light in our home, its warmth, its music. What a joy you made it for me to return there each night. Nor, try as they might, can our children appreciate your motherhood. For I was there during the pain of their beginning and I saw the years of concern that you never worried them to see.

The Lord made Eve to be Adam's helpmate. He made you to be mine. No prayer of thanksgiving could be sufficient.

We are just now approaching our winter yet in my heart it is still spring, for that's where you reside. I look at you now and I see the beautiful girl you were. I look at you now and see the beautiful wife, mother, grandmother you are. Your journey has been triumphant and I am so grateful you shared it with me.

Sid

ḣer feelɩŋgs

Anniversaries are celebrations and renewals. Each one is special. Once you could buy little booklets available at greeting-card shops and gift stores that listed each anniversary up to the 75th, describing its significance: from paper, iron, and pewter to silver, gold, and diamond, and listing appropriate gifts as well. No one seems to pay much attention to any such protocol these days. Few couples make it to a golden anniversary; fewer still reach the diamond anniversary. Some never make it to paper. Those who continue in their relationships have good reason to celebrate: their children, their growth and successes, their goals achieved, their problems solved, their griefs shared, their joys magnified. They also have every right to celebrate their staying power.

Costly gifts needn't be exchanged on an anniversary, no

matter what the "book" says. My father and mother burned their mortgage on one anniversary. One couple I knew planted a small flowering tree each year. Another couple didn't have much money. The first one to say "Happy Anniversary" got the one gift they could afford. She knew he let her say it first each time. In later years, they prospered and the gifts were mutual, but she still keeps the mementos of those first years. Others exchange gifts that have no money value—a pledge to perform a chore, an agreement to participate in something the other particularly enjoys. Some couples renew their marriage vows in a full ceremony, with family and friends in attendance, reemphasizing their faith and the solemnity of their union.

You needn't wait for marriage to celebrate an anniversary. Even if you are not overly sentimental and don't articulate your feelings easily, you may want to acknowledge the anniversary of your first meeting, your first date, or your first year together as a couple. Your remembrance doesn't have to be elaborate; it can be as simple as a single flower, a walk in the park where you met, or a dinner at the restaurant where you had your first date. Such tokens tell your partner that all the time you have spent together is momentous and reason for joy and celebration.

ḥer Lecter

Dear . . .

Just a small hotel—in Croton. Here's our reservation. I was worried that they might have closed. It's been so long.

The other day when I told you I visited Clare, it wasn't quite the whole truth. We drove up the Hudson and had lunch. We also drove through the area and there it was—still as picturesque—and much improved. You won't have to rely on the lake breezes this time: the bridal suite (right! the bridal suite) and every other room is air conditioned now. Better still, there's a restaurant right next door and Lake View Inn is still going strong. Just in case though, I checked on room service—available 24 hours. We may never go out to eat.

Remember, they think we're newlyweds, so I want you to act as nervous as you were ten years ago. You can tug your tie and wipe your forehead. Do you remember "Boy, it's hot in here" or "Gosh, it's hot in here"? It was. But you were hotter. All to no avail. I was so sunburned that we spent our honeymoon in the shower. This time I'm bringing a quart of sun screen #30. The only heat will be between us and we'll give the air conditioning a run for its money.

Linda

P.S. | When you write your anniversary love letter:

Do tell your partner of the many happy memories you have of the year that has just passed (or the week or month) and of the many you hope to create in the years to come.

Do suggest re-creating the event you are celebrating. An anniversary provides the opportunity to recall your first blissful times together.

Don't worry if you can't afford a gift. The gift of love is the most important gift and, ultimately, the only one that counts.

| C | H | A | P | T | E | R | 5 | 2 |

On Valentine's Day

You make me smile with my heart . . .
—Lorenz Hart, "My Funny Valentine"

There'll be no one but you for me, eternally,
If you will be my love . . .
—Sammy Cahn, "Be My Love"

ḣis ƒeeLiṅgs

Valentine's Day is my national holiday! Would you expect anything less of a hopeless romantic? Imagine one whole day dedicated to expressing your love for all who are dear to you. Until you have been my sweetheart on Valentine's Day, you have no idea what that day can mean. (See Chapter 58, "The Three-Dimensional Love Letter.") And whatever else I may do to show that special someone she's my Valentine, I always take time to write her a Valentine's Day love letter.

There are a host of stories about how the day began. They range from the day birds began to choose their mates to commemorating the martyrdom of a priest who secretly presided over the marriages of Christians despite an edict by the Emperor Claudius banning such weddings and was beheaded for his efforts. Whatever its origins, today it is a day for lovers—a day to be celebrated to the hilt.

Of course, it is not just a day for lovers. It is for anyone who truly cares for another and wants to let them know it. For example, I've always made Valentine's Day special for my daughter, Sherry ("my daughter, the teacher"). Others may come in and out of my life but Sherry is my forever Valentine.

For those who are seeing more than one person at a time, Valentine's Day can present a problem. That evening you can really only take out one date and so a choice has to be made. That's okay. At least once a year you should have to choose, should have to commit. And what better day than this?

But for true lovers there is no day to compare. The day was made especially for you. Open your hearts to the fullest. Tell her in a way she will never forget.

bis Letter

My darling . . .

Today is Valentine's Day, our day, a day created just for us. It's a day that celebrates love and lovers and, therefore, it must be our day. Surely no other fellow in the history of the world ever loved a girl as much as I love you. And no other guy was as lucky to be loved back.

I have this feeling that love was invented by us for no other feeling I've ever had compares to what I feel for you. I want the love that's bursting inside of me to light up the sky so you can see how true it is. True enough to last a lifetime.

Since I've never had a Valentine as important to me as you are, today I've pulled out all the stops. By the time you come home and get this letter, you will have received flowers and balloons and a candy heart. And if you check the bottom of the first page of the morning newspaper, you'll see a notice letting the whole world know:

> *"A___*
> *This day was made for us.*
> *Happy Valentine's Day.*
>   *Love,*
>   *Sid"*

You've brought such joy to my life and a tenderness I've never known. You've given me an excitement and a peace, a desire to improve and a contentment with who I am. I feel that with you all things are possible and, truly for the first time in my life, I fear nothing. Buoyant, that's the word I've been searching for— buoyant—loving you I float across the sea of life, over the bounding main, reveling in the sunshine of happiness.

In just a little while I'll call for you for our special night on the town. After a day of "fireworks," I've chosen a very quiet, beautiful restaurant in the Village. It has flowers and candlelight and romantic music. And if I've "shouted" my love for you all day long, tonight I'll whisper it—all night long.

Today is Valentine's Day but, in a larger sense, so long as you love me every day is Valentine's Day.

Happy day, happy love, happy life—together!
                        Sid

ḥer ƒeeliṇgs

Cards with lacy hearts and sweet sentiments. Red satin hearts filled with fancy chocolates. Heart-shaped earrings, pendants, pins. Even nightgowns and jockey shorts with little hearts. Corny? A little embarrassing even? Once you probably didn't think so.

Remember your first Valentine's Day in school? Receiving many wistful clumsily scrawled cards, or only a few, maybe a special one you hoped was from "*him.*" Who could tell? Every card was signed, "Guess who?" You hoped nonetheless. On your desk you drew a heart with an arrow through it, enclosing your initials and his.. You gave him tiny colored candy hearts with tinier messages: "Be mine." "Always." "All my love."

Why all the heart symbols? The heart was long considered the seat of emotion, the heart's blood to contain the perfect essence of life and love. And we still accept the symbol. Our hearts are touched, warmed, and won by love. They pound, throb, or ache with the excitement and sweet anguish of love. They are made of gold, they are hot and cold, dear and sweet, broken or whole. The heart has its own desires and delights. We seem to accept our hearts as having an existence apart from us, or at least from our minds. And we accord our hearts one day of celebration, whether we think of it as corny or cute, whether we buy the card, the candy, or small gift with a slight sense of foolishness or with "all our heart." Who's to say you can't give a guy candy, a flower? At least a card. You don't want him standing by the mailbox like Charlie Brown. This is a day set aside for lovers. Seize the day. Tell him how much you love him.

ḥer Leccer

Dearest . . .

Under all this lace and crepe paper you will find my heart (reasonable facsimile thereof). Please be assured that you have the original—even though it can't be taken out of its original package. Here are some hugs and kisses too—XXXXXOOOOO.

If you follow the trail of candy hearts when you come home tonight, you'll find some real lace waiting. No red crepe paper. The color tends to come off on your hands when it gets wet.

Best of all you can have my heart and the rest of the original packaging. All yours.

Can't wait. Happy Valentine.

Love,

Linda

P.S. | When you write to your sweetheart on Valentine's Day:

Ah, c'mon. We don't have to tell you anything about Valentine's Day. The reminders are everywhere. And you don't have to wait until February 14th!!

C H A P T E R   5 3

In the Dead of Winter

Rise up, my love, my fair one, and come away.
For lo, the winter is past, the rain is over and gone;
The flowers appear on the earth,
the time of the singing of birds is come,
and the voice of the turtle is heard in our land.
                                        —Ecclesiastes 2:10–12

his feelings

n those areas of the world where winter means cold and snow,
freezing winds and icy rains, most of society turns inward.
There are some compensations: parties and theater, outdoor
sports for the hearty and blazing fireplaces that encourage snug-
gling. But as the dreary days linger on, they can begin to affect our
entire outlook.

I've found that a loving letter creates more warmth than even a
crackling fire and brings with it renewed hope and optimism.

I enjoy reaching out to my sweetheart when the chill winds of winter
blow with the warm breath of romance, with the hot breath of desire.

his Letter

Dearest . . .

The storm continues to rage. It has been howling outside most of the week and the snow is well past the window sills. Although I have the thermostat set higher than my math marks in school, still the wind has found every crack and crevice and I'm sitting here in bundling. The wood's been used up and the fireplace taken early retirement. The only exercise I'm getting is at the typewriter but the book is going so slowly even my fingers are falling asleep. The only thing this weather is good for is daydreaming.

I close my eyes and remember us on the lake last spring, the breeze-blown sails, the water splashing, your laughter filling the boat with music. Fade out, fade in and we are picnicking on the great Tanglewood lawn listening to Rampal. . . You stretched out in the warm summer sun and I kissing you gently, repeatedly. Then autumn and the splendid colors of the Mohawk Trail, hiking through the woods, the leaves crunchy beneath our feet. Suddenly the chill is gone. Memories of you have warmed me as nothing else could have.

If only you were here now, we'd teach that fireplace a thing or two of heat and the only log that counted would never disappoint. Nor would either of us have cause to complain of the lack of exercise!

The days are short; they pass in boredom. The nights are endless. Thank Heavens winter's not. Ultimately it will end and we'll set about creating memories anew.

Rest assured my love for you is not hibernating. It is as alive as ever—the only truly warm thing in this forsaken outpost!

Glory be to love—and to you.

Sid

ber feeliⴖgs

The course of true relationships doesn't run smooth. You and your partner will confront minor and major problems together. With tenacity and courage, you can face problems such as moves that leave family and friends behind, loss of a job, or temporary financial difficulties and overcome them, still together and with your love intact. Major changes—the birth of children or their ultimate departure from home, severe illness, midlife crises, adultery, or the death of a loved one—can have severe effects on a relationship, even straining it to the breaking point. Even greater effort is required from both partners to preserve equilibrium during such life changes.

A different sort of crisis can occur in any long relationship. A chill sets in, a long cold season precipitated, it seems, by no really good cause. The thrill is gone. So is spontaneity and affection. The partners are polarized, either resentfully though silently isolated from each other or openly hostile.

What causes this dead cold state of affairs between once happy, devoted, and loving couples? Some people insist that it is inevitable, that mere long living together must result in contempt and distaste for each other. Others suggest that long-term involvements or marriages should involve a "reup," a reenlistment after two or three years if everything is going great, and voluntary termination without recrimination if it is not. None deny the possibility that winter might set in within two days after reenlistment or in two or three years with a new partner. And it very well might.

Yet such cold spells occur only if sunshine and warmth leave your relationship. You can avoid them. First, talk to each other, and keep talking. Voice your needs to each other, don't repress them. Don't let minor differences and disagreements become major by becoming part of a silent conspiracy. Second, be with

323

each other. Share time. Reserve part of each day to spend together even if the time is brief. Third, comfort and console each other. Any problem either partner has involves the other. Try to internalize your partner's feelings and to acknowledge your own role in the matter. Above all, love each other. Remember the love that brought you together and that has kept you together this long. Speak it out loud, and often. If you do, winter won't last. And Spring is around the corner.

ḣer Letter

Dearest . . .

I am writing this letter to ask you to come home. I'm torn up and frightened by my own request. But we've been apart for two months now and I'm not happier without you. I want you to come home to try to work it out and get past it.

I wish I could say I understand, but I don't. So many people say that at least three people take part in adultery: the couple and the "stranger." If I played a role in this, I don't know what it was. You always seemed happy in our marriage, happy and excited with our lovemaking.

People also say that most men and many women are adulterous at some time in their loves. But more men—" that's how men are." That's not how you are. I don't believe that—and that is why this has been so hard to credit, so hard to absorb.

If someone else had told me about it, I wouldn't have believed it. I would have wondered why they chose to say such cruel things to me. But you were the one to tell me. And that is why I want to try to make things good between us again. You deceived me for several months, but you couldn't continue in the deception. This is the fact that gives me hope—that renews my faith in you. Trust is hard won for me. My trust in you is abused but not lost.

I wish I could say I forgive and forget. That would be a lie and lies, not your act, are what almost destroyed us. Nothing can live that is based on lies.

If you want to come back—with this knowledge, I want you to, but I want something more. I want you to agree to talk this out with me. Then, if we don't solve it between us, I want us to see a therapist together. Then—who knows? But let's try.

Linda

P.S. | Whether it's the season or the state of your relationship to which you are referring, when you write in the dead of winter:

Do write a love letter at any time if for no other reason than to tell of your love. By doing so, you can keep the cold away forever.

Do remember that a love letter can warm the cockles of the coldest heart and create roaring fires from flickering embers.

Do acknowledge any difficulties that exist (your personal winter), if they do exist, and promise to do your best to resolve them. Acknowledge your role in them. Assure your partner of your caring and concern, your continued support, and the enduring quality of your love.

Don't turn away from each other when you are faced with difficulties. Crisis in any form assaults both of you. In such times, you need to know that there is at least one person on whom you can depend for aid and consolation . . . and warmth.

On Groundhog's Day

And young and old come forth to play
On a sunshine holiday.
    —John Milton, *L'Allegro*

To laugh is proper to man.
    —François Rabelais, *Gargantua and Pantagruel*

his feelings

f you have a sense of humor and great affection, any occasion can provide an opportunity to write a love letter. Sometimes these unexpected letters are the most appreciated. I've written love letters on Millard Fillmore's birthday, the day the Panama Canal was opened, and not infrequently on Groundhog's Day. Actually, that's a particularly good day to write a love letter.

Read the next and I think you'll see why.

his Letter

Dear . . .

The newscaster just said that Pauxatawny Phil saw his shadow today and scurried back into his hole. Three cheers for Phil and Happy Groundhog's Day!

My copy of the Farmers' Almanac says if the groundhog sees his shadow it means that spring is just 6 weeks away, The end of the long, cold winter is in sight. Soon quiet walks along the beach, tennis until we drop, robins (!), rides out into the country, and stopovers at quaint country inns.

I love spring—the season of rebirth when the whole world comes alive again. You, you are my spring. The winter of my own discontent had frozen my feelings until you came into my life. The warmth of your love melted my heart and through you I, too, came alive again. Therefore, for me each spring is our anniversary and I can't wait to celebrate it with you—all spring long.

Sid

P.S. | When you write a love letter on a "non-holiday":

Do pick this day or any other day, actual or nonexistent, to celebrate your love. Make up an occasion, call it Mammy Yokum Day or Hokum Day. Name it for your favorite literary character or your favorite position.

Do have fun with it.

On the Last Day of Summer

I will not let thee go.
Ends all our month-long love in this?
Can it be summed up so—
Quit in a single kiss?
I will not let thee go.
—Henry Brooks Adams, "Last Day of Summer"

ḣis ḟeeliṅgs

Some of the disparagement of summer romances is non-sense; some makes a lot of sense.

Summer is, perhaps, the easiest season to meet new people. The weather is generally beautiful, the setting is almost always informal, we are actively doing things we truly enjoy, and our attention is directed outward. Whether on the tennis court or around the pool, in the Hamptons or walking along the Marginal Way, fishing out of Islamorada or riding a bicycle down Haleakala—summer and sociability go hand in hand. And if you can't fall in love dancing under the stars on a warm summer's evening or sitting on the lawn at a Michael Feinstein concert, when can you fall in love?

On the other hand, everyday cares and concerns are left behind while on vacation and it is probably true that most of us are significantly different away from the office. It's at least possible that the person we've fallen in love with while on holiday is not the person we'll encounter when we see them again "in the city"— back home.

Such thoughts must be in the mind of every person who has enjoyed a summer romance as summer comes to a close.

If you really do intend to carry your romance back into town and on into the fall, it is a wonderful idea to take the occasion of the end of summer to write her and let her know what the summer has meant to you. It is an appropriate time for some reassurance.

ḥis Lecter

Dearest . . .

Magical—that's the only way to describe this summer.

Although we had met some months before it began, it was during the summer that you and I became an "us." How I looked forward to each long weekend together! The work days couldn't pass fast enough until we were in the car heading out to the shore. And when we were both able to take two weeks off and stay out there, I was so excited I couldn't sleep the whole night before we left.

And, oh, the memories as I reflect on the times we shared. Bike riding down the tree-lined lanes, playing tennis and lazying down by the pool, volleyball on the beach and late night cookouts, trying the newest little restaurant everyone seemed to discover simultaneously, and dancing the night away at this disco or that.

I remember simple things: holding your hand as we strolled through the village, sharing an ice cream soda after the movies, shopping for "supplies" for the house. I remember the day I thought you had gotten lost when we were riding through the woods and how I rushed up the stairs and held you in my arms, so grateful to find you had taken another path and simply gotten home before me. I remember the night we sat by the lake and talked about someday having a family. Golden days of hope. Starlit evenings of tender love. Was there ever such a summer before?

Soon we'll be packing everything up and heading home. One thing I'll be sure not to leave behind is my love for you. No, that I will wrap ever so carefully and carry with me back into the city. There, with equal care, I'll unwrap and polish it. Polish it so it will continue to sparkle through the months that lie ahead.

The season will change but not the way I feel about you. That will never change. Something happened this summer—something that made two people one—it was . . .

Magical. And that's the way it will remain.

Sid

P.S. | When you write on the last day of summer:

Do consider your partner. We assume you both know the conditions of your relationship, its recent history and potential future (or lack of one). If you were both having fun and games, stress the fun and good memories.

*Do l*et your partner know if you want the relationship to continue. This is a time for reassurance that it was more than casual. . . if, in fact, it was more than casual.

Don't hurt the other person even if summer wasn't the hottest ever.

Don't be bound by September 21st (or 22nd—we can never remember which). It's always nice to let someone know you enjoyed the season, whenever it occurs.

CHAPTER 56

On the Birth of a Child

> *Love set you going like a fat gold watch . . .*
> *you try your handful of notes;*
> *The clear vowels rise like balloons.*
> — Sylvia Plath, "Morning Song"

his feelings

We had just graduated school and moved to a new town. We had a ten-year-old car, $34 in savings, and she was 8 1/2 months pregnant. My employers briefed me on their health plan. It didn't kick in for the first month! Oh, child, be late—be late! The days passed slowly. We kept our fingers crossed.

I remember we went to the supermarket and filled the basket to the brim. Waiting at the checkout counter, Joyce turned to me and said quietly, "I don't think we're going to have time for this." Indianapolis never had a driver who drove faster than I did through the streets of Rochester, New York. We got there in no time flat. And then the waiting began.

The doctors let me stay with my wife for most of the labor but then directed me to the waiting room. It would be many years before medicine would recognize the "value" of allowing a husband to stay by his wife's side throughout.

Some hours later (it seemed like years), the doctor came out, told me that Joyce was doing fine, and that we had a son! A son! And just past midnight. A paid-for son! I rushed to her side, kissed her forehead and told her she never looked more beautiful. In truth, she never had.

Our families were hundreds of miles away. After all the phone calls had been made, I drove home, sat in our sparsely furnished apartment and cried. Joy, relief, anxiety—all the emotions flooded out. It was 4:30 A.M. I had to be at work in just four hours. I picked up a pen and wrote the new mother a letter. . .

bis Letter

Dearest . . .

If there were a medal of honor for new mothers, I'd drive back to the hospital and pin it on your nightgown. You were so brave tonight and the doctor said that continued even after they made me leave. He said that in every way possible you were the perfect delivering mom.

And what a beautiful son you gave us! There wasn't a mark on him and I swear he smiled the moment he saw me. While the nurse was completing her records, he asked such intelligent questions about the new Federal Rules of Procedure. I told you I thought he'd be a lawyer.

Lawyer, teacher, mechanic, businessman—let him be whatever he wants so long as he's happy. But someday may he find a girl as wonderful as his father found and may she be as fine a wife to him as you have been to me.

A son . . . someone to bear my dad's name. I'll never be able to thank you for that.

Have you ever noticed that all newborn babies clench their fists? I guess they know it can be a tough world and want to come out fighting. I want to help create an environment for our son in which his fists don't have to be clenched, one in which he is surrounded by love and kindness and caring.

That's one lucky child you've brought into this world. He's got the best mother any kid ever had and a dad who loves them both more than anything. For you and for Michael, I'll work hard and be provident; I'll be loving and supportive; I'll try to be wise and I'll always be generous and kind.

Congratulations, Mommy! You are a very, very special person and I've never been prouder of you—nor more in love.

Sid

P.S. | When you write to your beloved on the birth of your child:

Do tell your partner of your love, now so specially enhanced by living proof of your love for each other.

Don't let your love for each other abate in the slightest as your face your new responsibilities. The best security for any child is the love that child's parents have for each other.

On the Marriage of Our Daughter

*Let all thy joys be as the month of May
And all thy days be as a marriage day . . .*
—Frances Quarles, "To a Bride"

his feelings

don't remember a time when Sherry wasn't planning her wedding. I think she had the colors picked out before she learned to ride a two-wheeler. All little girls seem fascinated with brides and weddings and the like. Most big girls, too.

What a day this will be for the family. I don't think we'll find a hall large enough to hold her mother's pride. Being the father of the bride, that's a title I wouldn't trade for Prince of the Realm either.

Just before the wedding is a great time to let your own bride know how you feel about her—and the unique role she played in raising your daughter. It's one of those occasions that cry out for an extra sentimental touch.

hIS LETTER

Dearest . . .

Tomorrow our "little" girl will walk down the aisle "all dressed in white." It's a day we've talked about almost from the day she was born. And it's finally here.

That young man of hers is surely one of the luckiest fellows alive. He's getting a most extraordinary woman—bright, beautiful and balanced. The happiest, most enthusiastic person I know. Upbeat, kind, generous, and creative. A super citizen of any community in which they settle. And what a mother she'll make. Just listen to me go on. You'd think I was the father of the bride.

Well, that's a pretty good role but it's not what this letter is all about. No, this is about the mother of the bride. Just as bright, beautiful and balanced. In fact, all the wonderful things I see in our daughter are things I've always seen in you. She is, of course, her own person but she is also so much of you.

I know that being a mother was not easy. You did so much of it alone when I was off hither and yon—and you built your own career in the process. But you succeeded brilliantly nonetheless. I've always admired your high standards and your values: standards and values your folks gave you in far simpler times. Yet you transmitted them intact to our daughter despite the tensions and complexities of the times of our lives.

Tomorrow it's a safe bet that everyone will be looking at the bride. I will, too. But when I look at that bright and beautiful vision in white, I'll be seeing another bride. The one who walked down

338

*an aisle with me, July 7th, 1963—the most special day of my life.
You've done it all, girl, and I love you for it. Even if tomorrow
you do become a mother-in-law!*
Sid

P.S. | When you celebrate your daughter's wedding with a love letter:

Do remind your spouse of the reason you are attending this wedding: your spouse.

Do reaffirm your love for each other as you share this joyful occasion.

Don't let any personal problems (even divorce) mar this most joyous day for your child. She is just beginning. She needs to see the two of you united in love for her.

CHAPTER 58

The Three-Dimensional Love Letter

"**W**ords, words, words," complained Eliza Doolittle to Freddy Eyensford-Hill, the moonstruck young man enamored of her. "Don't speak to me of words—SHOW ME!"

Great advice. Words are important, or we wouldn't have written a book encouraging you to communicate more fully and more effectively, but words are not equal to actions. The hurt that our thoughtless actions cause can rarely be assuaged merely by the use of words. Conversely, if our actions consistently manifest care and concern, they speak more effectively of our love than all the sonnets ever written.

If you love someone, tell him or her—both with your words and your deeds. On occasion, do the chore he or she would normally do but finds distasteful: the dishes, the laundry, running this or that errand, making the bed. Not very romantic stuff, you say? Helping out is a wonderful way to express love. So is the unexpected courtesy. If you're a man, rise when she approaches the table in a restaurant or when she leaves it, open the door, help her on with her coat. The struggle for equal rights should mean assuring women equal access to all that society offers; it doesn't mean forsaking consideration or good manners. If you're a woman, offering to split the check, getting the theater tickets for both of you, or going along with him to an event you'd just as soon skip are really nice ways of saying, "I care"—and a lot more effective.

Flowers (or helium-filled balloons) are a wonderful expression of your love. We send them all the time. Before a special date, with the card:

> *Tonight, tonight won't be just any night.*
> *I can't wait!*

On the occasion of a promotion:

> *I believe in you . . .*
> *And obviously I'm not the only one.*

For her birthday, a rose for every year:

> *One for every hundred times I think of you.*
> *One for every thousand times I love you.*

But flowers or balloons shouldn't only be sent on special occasions. Send them for no particular reason at all other than the chance to let her know:

> *I care.*

Nor are flowers something only to be sent from a man to a woman. Since most men don't expect them, they are an extra special surprise.

Gifts are another way of expressing love. They needn't be reserved for special occasions and they needn't be big. When you are off on a business trip, an appropriate memento you bring home shows the one you love that he or she was missed and remembered. Recall your sweetheart saying he was looking for a particular item you've just found? Get it for him. The message is simple: "I listen. I hear. I care." And you need never express it in words. Know of something she wants but hasn't been willing to get for herself? That's a super gift idea.

One of the most well-received gifts Sid recalls giving was a framed collage of mementos he secretly saved from their dates: a match cover, a wine label, a restaurant review, ticket stubs, dried flowers. Nan loved it. Last Valentine's Day, he had a star named after Lynn and presented her with a framed map of the Heavens showing the location of "her" star. There's a company that does that for you. It brought tears to her eyes because it signalled that their friendship was eternal. And when he re-encountered his high school sweetheart after a lifetime apart, he sent her 34 handcrafted Valentines—one for each year they'd missed—even though the month was August. He's forever sending Myra books. She has a whole shelf in her library just holding "Sid sent me" books, and for his last birthday she got him a necktie with the logo of his favorite restaurant. (She reads, he dines?) And jade, always jade, for, as the Chinese believe, a part of the giver's soul goes with a gift of jade.

Linda suggests, when the time is right, giving your loved one a key ring—together with a key to your door. Nice touch.

Records or tapes of the concert you've just seen will bring back the memory forever. And there's always that special food. There are even stores that will make gifts out of chocolate!

Remember, the gift doesn't have to be fancy but it must say, "I know who you are and I chose something with your happiness in mind."

Some three-dimensional gifts can be more elaborate. For example, there is an electronic billboard in Times Square, New York City. You can have your message put up there for one minute at any time of day you specify and get an 8"x10" color photo. Sid remembers having a friend join him from Florida to be greeted by:

> *Michaella,*
> *I'm falling in love with you.*
> *Sid*

As she later wrote him, "Times Square will never be the same again!"

For even less, you can hire a student from a local music school to stand in her lobby or outside her door, or visit her office, and play a romantic song on the violin for Valentine's Day.

Don't forget charity, either. If you know a cause your loved one is committed to, a donation in their honor is an awfully nice way to say, "I not only love you. I honor you." Andra thinks that's probably the nicest gift.

What is a "three-dimensional love letter?" It is any way other than words of expressing your devotion. We encourage loving communication. We also encourage loving acts.